TOKENS
of
LOVE

The Provenance, Purposes and Constituents of English Needlework Samplers. Explaining samplers of Poor Girls, and their life in Poor and Orphan Schools.

by Vivian Crellin

"When I was young and quite untaught
These letters I with needle wrought;
Bit when I'm older and know more,
I'll make them better than before."
Sewn on the sampler of Mary Gay. 1808

Tokens of Love

is

published by The Sampler Guild,
19 York Road, Maidenhead, Berkshire. SL6 1SQ
www.thesamplerguild.co.uk

© Vivian Crellin, November 2006
ISBN 0-9554672-0-9
ISBN 978-9554672-0-2

"You'll mend your life tomorrow, still you cry
In what far country does this morrow lie?
It stays so long, 'tis fetched so far, I fear,
'Twill both be very old and very dear."
Sewn on the sampler of M.M., aged 8, 1790

CONTENTS

ACKNOWLEDGEMENTS

In sale rooms and museums; in homes where lovers of Needlework Samplers dwell; from innumerable conversations, advice and demonstrations, I have come to understand my subject better.

Printed works consulted are named in a Bibliography at the end of the book. Of all those who helped and encouraged me, there are some to whom I am personally indebted.

Kay and Anthony Scaramanga, who once bought, sold, knew and loved the finest samplers on the market. Their friendship was a delight.

Joy Jarrett of Witney Antiques, who showed me in her remarkable store so much of the story that samplers have to tell.

Carol Humphrey of the Fitzwilliam Museum, in token of many museum curators who showed their collections to me.

Dorothy Phelan, the first to undertake a critical and wise correction of the typescript. With kindly thoroughness she pointed out errors that blushed for shame.

Jacqueline Holdsworth who advised recasting the emphasis and chapters.

And especially, Linda Hadden, founder of The Sampler Guild, whose enthusiasm brought about publication when others showed courteous unwillingness to read the script.

I would, if I could, thank thousands of sampler makers who beguiled the world with the spirit of childhood. I can and do thank the girl I met first when we were both very young, for magically, she is still with me. She taught me how to love and to be loved. In this book and by many precious tokens, she crowned a youth invaded by war; and enabled me to renew its irresponsible joys.

This book is dedicated to my wife, Eileen.

INTRODUCTION

"You ask me why I love, go ask the glorus son
why it throw the world doth run
ask damask roses why so full they blow
and all things suckets fesh   (fresh sweetmeats)
which forceeth me to love"

from the Sampler of Elizabeth Matrom 1718. Fitzwilliam Museum.

Remembrance of childhood is an aching, sweet thing. Once upon a time most schoolchildren shared the belief that their birth ushered in an age of such shining light that day-to-day punishment was but a small price to pay for the riches of the world around them. They were used to summary punishment.

Few children at school before the Second World War escaped the punishment of Writing Lines.

We scribbled, "I must not write on the blackboard", or a similar finger-wagging admonition; and we had to do it a hundred times. It was so boring! Time dragged, and pens clogged with inky hairs; but when it was done we were released out of the classroom with joy, and never wrote on the blackboard again unless we were certain sure we could get away with it.

It was easier to supervise detention by giving naughty children something to do. But, long before those days, Copy-Lines had not been a punishment: they were then the only way schoolchildren were taught to write perfectly with pen and ink.

For a thousand years, schoolchildren learned to use a pen by copying the script of a line the teacher had written at the Heading of the page. A faithful copy was written, ten times only or the work would be sure to fail. Painstakingly the children copied the shape of the master's letters. Tongues peeped from the corners of the mouth in tense concentration needed to get the angles and loops of junctions exactly done. With a final flourish to show the fluid elegance of English Round Hand, the words were formed.

The sentences copied were short enough to fill a line, and as punchy as an advertisement. In those concentrated hours of copying, what the pupil took subliminally into his mind was always a moral axiom.

Few Copybooks have survived from medieval times and copybook methods were abandoned after the First World War. Close study of 17th to 19th century copybooks give a fascinating glimpse into long dead schoolrooms.

The copy-lines that were passed traditionally from one Writing-Master to another spoke of a real adult world; of getting on with people, and the arts of striving for success.

They urged no submission to piety; nor taught the salvation of souls in another world, but advised living decently in this. All together, they composed a complete moral philosophy that was not at all Christian. The Copybook Headings were drawn from the sayings of wise Cato, a heathen Stoic of Classical Rome.

When I first came to this conclusion, I tossed off the thought that the Copybook Headings were not at all like the verses English girls sewed in their samplers. But considering how few samplers I had seen, I decided to study all the samplers I could find and see if the difference truly existed.

For years I looked closely at the details of Needlework Samplers, and studied books others had written. After copying thousands of sampler verses, from sales, auctions, private collections, museums, and galleries the precise difference became clear. By this chance I came to know and love samplers; yet still I am wary of intrusion.

Like a newcomer kindly welcome, fascinated and gladdened by a feminine world, I may unravel the complexity of stitches, images and symbols to read the patient beauty and meaning expressed in samplers. It is no more than an interpretation of their history. But in writing of young girls in the delicate rush of their emerging awareness, I hesitate before a creature I have never been.

The help and encouragement of those already acknowledged has brought me to it now. What prompted me to begin was the first serious piece of needlework I ever did.

One year, when the kids had finished their exams, and summer holidays released us, we drove to stay on the Isle of Skye.

A family of eagles circled one of the peaks, riding the up-currents and tumbling the air in mock pursuit; as unafraid of death and satisfied with life as I had been barrel-rolling through the clouds when the war was over. In the years between, I had taught a lot of wonderful, brave and lovely children, and had come to the mountains for a rest.

Looking down from high rocks, I saw far Eilean Donan and the ferry that had carried us over the sea. They were as dim and distant as childhood.

I knew then a little more about children than when I had been one, and lots more about needlework samplers.

Half way through the day, I came back off the ridge that looks down on the shadows of Loch Coriusk, my legs bitten into pimples by midges. I strode a sunlit valley between the red and the black Cullins; and as she saw me come, my wife released Bess who bounded through the heather and greeted me within sight of the inn at Sligachan.

That evening before dinner, I sat in the lounge with Eileen. My boots were outside, but otherwise I was still in climbing clothes, drinking gratefully from a seven-shilling beer. Lighting my pipe, I took up the needlework kit she had bought me. It copied the print of a wonderful American sampler. The original would have cost thousands.

I started to sew the patient, obedient stitches. Eileen smiled, so it was all right, even if slightly ridiculous. Others came in, and smiled or raised their eyebrows, but were too polite to comment. The sampler grew, and I began to enjoy it.

I'll never know exactly what it is like to be born a girl, but my heart was full of admiration for the samplers I had come to recognise, and for the little girls who made them.

Chapter 1.

SCHOOLS IN THE SAMPLER AGE

"Look well to what you take in hand,
For larning is better than house or land.
When land is gone and money spent
Then larning is most excellent."

Mary Canting, August 18, 1694. Fitzwilliam Museum

Needlework Samplers stitched by young English girls from 1600 C.E. to 1900 are poignant reminders of a world too distant to allow us more than an echo of their lives and expectations. Looking at them, we see the meticulous stitches; and imagination gently touches the purposes and pains of those who made them. Often their yearning hope was that, after their death, someone would find in these memorials the message they wanted us to understand.

A knowledge of embroidery helps. A loving sympathy for beautiful stitching grows. Knowledge of history sets the scene. Some samplers were made in the quiet republic of domestic sewing circles, where skill was respected and age or social position stood back to welcome each talent and new delight. Many more were made under a sterner tutelage, at school. For sure, those schools were unlike the ones we know today, and to understand the girls and their sewing, it is important to know their atmosphere and disciplines. We then can picture the home or school in which samplers were sewn.

Why do people so often demand that learning should be full of excitement? The truth is that most things we need to learn require determination and patience. Inspiration comes in precious flashes. Children in their lessons need to be calm. They get enough excitement anyway and it often ends in tears. Remember the best teachers who come back to your mind? The tone of their voices and the atmosphere of their quiet classes?   Learning spoke with authority, privately, to individual minds isolated from the crowd of companions all around.

Good teaching speaks to the class and reaches each receptive one of them. It was true of the sewing circle; and long, long ago it was necessary for the schooling of rich and poor in England. It is an un-dramatic history.

Until civilization dawned there had been no need for schools at all. Apart from walking and talking, skills which come by natural time and by copy, the most important things children need to know were taught by parents.

Mother and father taught their children how to be useful and courageous; to restrain selfish wants and think of others; to be polite and fit for the society of equals when they grow up. If children wanted a particular skill beyond a parent's talents, they were put apprentice to someone who had that skill and who taught by practice and example. Reading and Writing were the first skills that called for schooling.

Early Anglo-Saxon literature was remembered and sung. Written language largely began with the coming of Christian clergy and was with few exceptions confined to Latin. Monastic and Cathedral Schools taught boys who aimed for the life of a monk or a priest, but literary skill was also serviceable to the King for his law courts, and to record family or national concerns. Clergy, clerics, clerks, and lawyers, all began with the same studies.

It was a testing discipline, suitable only for the brightest minds.

The Church sought out boys with natural ability and love of Christian learning, whether rich or poor, and for them studies were a road to their ambitions. The Church also schooled abandoned and orphan children, some for the humbler duties of monastic life, singing their lessons in the Chantries, tending lands and gardens, or meticulously fashioning and painting letters on parchment books in the Scriptoria.

And what of girls?

Mothers who could read taught their daughters, much as they do today; for the ability to read opened doors to a woman's devotions and the world of Christian books and prayers. The ability to write was exceptional, a talent for determined minds; so women were generally restricted to the books that men had written, and only in persuasive speech could they influence others with the content of their own minds. They managed to do that remarkably well.

Some girls entered the nunneries, where, in a life of pious humility and patient duties they learned two subjects particularly - Reading and Needlework.

The embroidery of Saxon women was renowned throughout Europe. The nimble fingers of poor women in the Nunneries, and of the noblest ladies of the land in their castles conspired to bedeck the pretentious dress of men. The work of the English, Opus Anglicanum, was received with acclaim as gifts to kings, archbishops and popes who valued and preserved it with admiration. When Odo, the Bishop of Bayeux, wished to record the triumph of his kinsman William the Conqueror, he had a huge tapestry stitched by English women. The triumph of the Normans was recorded by the recognised excellence of Saxon women.

Bayeux Tapestry:
Embroidered by Saxon women, to decorate the palace of the Bishop of Bayeux. Medieval embroidery adorned the vestments of the clergy, clothed the gentry, and hung to separate bed-spaces and rooms in the draughty halls of the nobility. Its heraldry and marks of rank identified all families of distinction. The symbolism of the art was given lustre by threads of silk and precious metals.

Naturally, embroidery samplers would have been used to prepare the cleverest emblems, but they are gone and, anyway, the subject of this book is not adult work, but the samplers made by children as a particular and different task much later on in time.

In all those years, school teaching was by repetition and copy from perfect examples. Any personal talent had to appear by gradual mastery once those models came patiently within each child's grasp. Discipline was strict; comforts were Spartan; and the stone corridors rang with a joyless determination to master skills that would distinguish the children's future. Those without dedication dropped out. Play or folly found little room to invade more serious commitments.

The chances that brought bright children to notice, or threw them on the mercies of Charity passed most children by, and they were not schooled. It is wrong to suppose that the poor did not go to school; indeed, throughout medieval times, some poor children rose to the most powerful places in the kingdom. Likewise it is wrong to suppose the rich did go to school.

Noble families taught their children by tutors and governesses at home. They learned to ride, to hunt, to fight, and to command. For men, these were absolute necessities; and if, like Alfred the Great or Henry VI, boys were of a contemplative mind they were also taught to Read and Write. It was an attractive curiosity, but unnecessary so long as the family had servants enough for these conveniences. Yet, by 1500, literacy was such a social and useful skill that few of the nobility kept to their old rough ignorance of learning.

The habit of sending gentle-born children to serve in the houses of more powerful family and friends absorbed them in the learning and influence of great families. Good manners, skills, self command, discretion and social confidence were learned by a kind of osmosis as plants take up water.

Commoner's children seldom went to school. Most were engaged very busily helping the family to survive; scaring crows from the crops, taking geese to the common, washing and mending clothes, carrying firewood, looking after the smaller children or the sick, taking cattle to market, cooking, making ale, picking blackberries or mushrooms, sweeping the house, going errands, and looking for birds' eggs.

It was the middle orders of society that had the greatest need for schools. Schools had the advantage of gathering enough pupils of the same ability to make lessons efficient. Schools had teachers of sufficient authority to keep the noses of reluctant children to the grindstone of their lessons.

Even in comfortable families, children had little time to play, and must work as soon as they could walk. The work of boys and girls was essential to the economy of the home. Days began as the sun rose and ended with its setting. No! That's not true. "A man toils from sun to sun, but a woman's work is never done".

Families making their fortunes in trade had needs that were served by Grammar Schools, and more were founded in the fifteenth century in towns without Cathedral Schools. Most were founded as charities to teach eight or so poor boys and bring them up to be clerks or to go at fifteen years to a university to finish their schooling as priests. Many such schools also cared for an equal number of poor and old folk. It is in the nature of mankind that these charitable intentions did not last.

Church and Monastery Schools once supplied the small need there was for the poor to be literate. Considerable financial support for Ecclesiastical Schools had come from the custom of Obits; money bequeathed for the souls of the dead, to shorten the pangs of Purgatory. In thirty or so weeks following the burial, Chantry monks sang obituary prayers to ease the soul of the donor into Heaven. Only the rich made wills, and strong tradition encouraged bequests to pay for the church to perform this duty.

The Reformation ended all that. Protestants believed fiercely that God judged men by the merit of their lives, and not by the intercession of prayer after death. Rich men, when refused their Obits, took to building Charities to house a few old people or a few children, hoping to show their benevolence before God.

If the Foundation was for old people, the buildings were called Almshouses; if for the sick, they were called Hospitals; if for orphans, they were called Asylums; and if for children, they were called Schools. Many had multi-purposes and most had annual religious ceremonies praising before God the memory of their founders.

Teachers soon found that, if the supply of talented or needy folk at the beginning or end of their lives was insufficient, there were others who would pay to board children with them, to take advantage of generous charity buildings, and to learn from their teaching all that gentry or traders needed to know. That is how the "House" system of schools began.

Some parents wanted a full classical education, some a smattering of Latin. Most required thorough teaching of reading, writing, mathematics and command of the English language. Grammar Schools came to be divided into "Classical" and "Modern" sides.

The interior of an Elizabethan Boys' School:
Infants on their Forms read from a Horn Book; in a Writing Class a boy copies script; inkhorns hang up; Music notes are written on a blackboard; parents at the back see the disciplines of the school. A line of young boys waits to prove they can read from a book. The master supervises one great room, helped by ushers who take separate oral lessons. They administer punishment with the birch. The hubbub can be imagined. A girls' school would be quieter and more decorous.

When the Reformation wiped out monastery and nunnery schools, the foundation of new Grammar Schools to replace them became urgent. Shakespeare as a day boy at Stratford Grammar School was taught his "little Latin and no Greek" just as many others did who never expected to go on to university or the church.

Girl's schools came later and generally paid little attention to the classics or mathematics, so they were seldom Grammar or Foundation Schools. Girls went to private schools that taught Reading, Writing, Arithmetic and English along with lady-like accomplishments such as Dancing, French and Needlework.

An example of Tudor Needlework. Maidstone Museum:
An emblematic allegory of the Tudor Succession. Edward VI presents the English Prayer Book to his father, Henry VIII. The monasteries are underfoot and the papal crown kicked away. Elizabeth in Glorious sunlight shows her father's bible has triumphed under Protestant rule. Mary, mute under a cloud, has a Catholic rosary. Her pet dragon wears a papal mitre. The Rose of England; the Thistle of a Scots succession; Heartsease of Confidence and the basket of Plenty show prosperity. Tidings of great joy may refer to the defeat of the Spanish Armada, many years before this was sewn.
    Courtesy of Maidstone Museum & Bentlif Art Gallery.

Needlework Samplers from affluent families were made both at school and in the home. It is not always easy to know which.

By the restoration of Charles II in 1660, there were very few schools open to the poor, yet the need for literate labour had expanded hugely since the invention of printing. The education of gentle girls included the first steps of embroidery. Embroidery once declared the rank, and wealth of its owners, and was by law forbidden to the common people. The law, seldom enforced, faded from use, and successful tradesmen elbowed their way into gentility by affecting the fashionable distinction.

Before schools for girls had become common, in the sewing circles of rich and comfortable families the making of needlework samplers by young girls found a new importance.

Chapter 2.

PORE MEN'S MAYDEN CHILDREN

These works in hand my frinds may have when I in grave am laid.

O Lord I am not puft in mind; I have no scornful eye,
I do not exercise myself in things that be to high;
But as the child that wained is, even from his mother's breast,
So have I, Lord, behave myself in silence and in rest.

With what God sends let us contented rest
A little is anuf if truly blesst.

Anonymous sampler, 1709, Fitzwilliam Museum.

The abject poor could not afford needle and thread. They wore cast-offs. Their girls could not learn sewing, nor their letters and samplers at home.   Some, more hopeful families with a man in work, who were yet too poor to afford schooling, made shift to teach their children the useful and decorative skills of more comfortable families.

They made samplers of a sort that betray the difficulties they faced; with faults in the formation of letters, spelling and grammatical errors of a grosser sort, yet within a sampler that had the colour and style of confident hope. There will always be families who wish to improve their lives and social standing. Comparisons teach. The yearning to improve and to give children opportunities that parents were denied, are not unforgivable faults. People interested in the samplers of the poor need look beyond the exuberant designs of more fortunate families and find evidence of the children who made mean and faulty samplers. The poignant hopes and fears, the interruptions and doubts, and many of the hardships and duties were the same for daughters of all social classes.

They were just more daunting and shorter of remedy for the poor. Their meagre efforts, where they survive, are curious though lacking meticulous or imaginative skills.

"Then will I tell the sin
ners rounb what a bear
Savour i have founb and pint to
Thy re deming blood and say behold the
way to god"   Elizabeth Kempton age 13 Her Work 1843

"CAROLLOYFUL
CAROLFOr
THE COMING OF
CHRISTTHE
TIVITYAGE 12"   Annie Wade, 1906 (her alphabet sampler had J and L alike.)

Rich or poor, light indoors was seldom bright enough for fine needlework. Sewing was done by windows or in doorways, as lace-makers worked, to take what sunlight there was. At night, wax candles gave light enough for household tasks, but the tallow tapers of the poor were only sufficient to avoid bumping into things once outside the firelight. Both gave a yellow glow that strained the eye looking at small stitches, or the show of colour. A note pinned to Mary Dudden's sampler, 1785, records that part of it was sewn by moonlight.

Daylight hours were busy with duties, and it is remarkable that young children could sew their samplers so finely and diligently. The want of light was one of many difficulties standing in the way of the poor making samplers at all.

During the 18th Century, the poor had struggles enough to get improvement: girls had to surmount additional prejudices that distinguished them from boys. In private schools, girls were seldom taught Latin or Mathematics and Accounts. While boys did these subjects, girls learned simple domestic arithmetic, and of course, Needlework, which was an essential subject for them, rich or poor.

The style of teaching was also different. In the 19th Century, fortunate girls were taught to write Ladies' Angular Hand, so they should not be mistaken for shop-keepers. They were encouraged to write of the petty adventures and emotions of family life: boys wrote argumentative and philosophical essays where reason ruled. But fortunate girls did at least get the skill of writing, at school, or from tutors and governesses at home.

Before 1690 there were few schools available to the poor. With the first flush of the Renaissance, Christ's Hospital School was opened where a Greyfriars house had been suppressed in 1553. The school accepted "fatherless and pore men's mayden children", but its care and opportunities were later opened to more fortunate families. Few Grammar Schools kept to their founding obligation to find talent among the poor. Most schools saved themselves from decay by taking Private pupils into their Public buildings. It is from this circumstance that the most expensive and ancient schools in England are called "Public Schools", something that confuses foreigners trying to make sense of English education.

There were, in some villages and towns, Parish Schools that taught the poor freely. The quality of their teaching was dependent on local philanthropy; good in one place, cursory in another. Individual benefactors opened Orphanages, Foundling Hospitals and Schools, but none of this provision gave more than a patchy and slim chance poor children might be taught at all.

Poor Schools decayed. With confidence and subscriptions failing, most of them concentrated on apprenticeship; labour for poor boys, domestic service for girls. Some became factories, earning what they could from child labour. Few taught more than reading.   What was rare for boys was almost absent for girls.

In 1634 the common council of Bristol set up a committee "to consider of a meet woman with twelve young girles to be setled for a beginning in the new Hospitall of Mr Alderman Whitson's gifte." John Whitson had known poverty but, after a Grammar School classical education and hard times, he had prospered as a merchant. As alderman, mayor and respected benefactor, he helped restore the rocky finances of Bristol Grammar and Cathedral Schools, and was aware that there was little or no education for poor female children. His daughters died in childhood and his heart was touched by concern for girls who were exposed to poverty by the death of a father.

The School established by his will became known as the "Red Maids School" from the uniform of scarlet serge, white apron and bonnet. The girls shared six flock-filled beds, and a shilling "lookeing glasse". By 1843 the hospital had expanded to take 140 poor or fatherless girls. In all this time, sewing, singing and reading was all the education the children had, though every effort was made to maintain their proper care. Visitors were commissioned to examine the health and cleanliness of the girls; their diet, employment, and freedom from vermin. Girls found unclean or unwholesome were expelled, and later it was agreed that no child with any bodily imperfection or deformity should be admitted.

Punishment was usually by extra chores, missing supper, or periods of silence. Whipping, for the gravest faults, was rare. Corporal punishment was avoided by stripping girls of their red uniforms and standing them motionless on a stool in public gaze, dressed in rough penitential clothes. Some girls would have preferred a private thrashing to this humiliation. Most wardens could not bring themselves to administer corporal punishment.

By Whitson's will the Mistress was to have the proceeds of the girls' work. The girls were accepted at eight or ten years of age and effectively apprenticed to the Matron who was paid £3 a year for each child, and later more. She economised to make the employment pay. The character and ability of House-mothers shaped the lives of their pupils. Spinning or plain-sewing was the likeliest labour. It was unlikely the girls were taught to make samplers, and none survive.

Most girls were destined to apprenticeship as "housewives, weavers, sempstresses, broiderers, lace-making, silk-knitting" and the like. Training helped to make the girls good servants. Those who married straight from school might be given a "portion" for a dowry. Occasionally the school kept girls until as late as eighteen years of age; a situation that tested the ability of the mistress to keep the school from scandal.

The school of the Little Red Maids raised the lives of poor girls above starvation and despair. Difficulties and doubts that were tested in the history of the school ensured very few other towns had even that much to offer.

Then, in 1698, in a burst of philanthropic enthusiasm, the Society for Promoting Christian Knowledge was formed to build Charity Schools for the Poor. Its spring was the strength of the restored Church of England, and reaction to the dissolute morals which followed the restoration of Charles II. The SPCK was inspired to reclaim the moral spirit of poor children and, opposing the non-conforming and dissenting sects, to teach children the doctrines of the established church. "Poor" often excluded the rough, poorest of the poor, and was meant for the deserving poor; decent parishioners who could not afford to school their children privately. Charity Schools also welcomed the decent destitute, orphans and foundlings; who were innocent of being the cause of their own misfortune.

Another hope was to "improve" poor boys to take skilled places in the ships of our navies. They wished to copy the success of the Dutch who had taught our sailors such a sharp lesson in 1667. St Clement Danes Charity School taught its "Navigation Boys" Writing and Mathematics well enough to disappoint the aim of the founders and fit them for lucrative posts more attractive than the sea service. Generous teaching at a Charity School in Great Ayton allowed the son of a farm labourer to find employment in commerce and to become the greatest navigator of his time. James Cook, ill at ease in the highest society of learned men, was honoured by those who valued his achievements above the reticence that betrayed his origins.

St Clement Danes, was one of the earliest SPCK schools and admitted girls in 1702. The poor boys were given uniform blue jackets, waistcoats and corduroy trousers; the girls, straw bonnets, blue check dress and cape. They wore their uniform with pride and gave public display of their confidence. All were taught to read, write and cast accounts; very much the same curriculum that would have been suitable for the children of tradesmen in local Private Schools. It was in such Charity Schools that most of the samplers of the poor were made.

The sampler of Mary Windom, begun in 1723, has the Anchor symbol of Hope, which was the emblem of the school. It has the "Boxers" of an earlier time, and figures of a lady and gentleman, perhaps subscribers or teachers of the school. These motifs and the following pious sentences had been the established tradition of samplers there since 1712.

"HE THAT GIVETH TO THE POOR LENDETH TO THE LORD AND HIS REWARD WILL BE IN HEAVEN"

"BE NOT WISE IN THINE OWN EYES. FEAR THE LORD AND DEPART FROM EVIL".

The colourful generosity of this sampler is unrestrained by any doubts: The charity children were given the teaching and style subscribers would have expected for their own children. This generosity was not shown in all other schools, and some were far more grudging in their charities. Charity Schools and enthusiasm for their support declined sharply until few withstood the desire to restrain rather than raise the expectations of poor children.

Mary Windom's sampler, sewn in 1723 at St Clement Danes.
A Charity School for orphaned and destitute children. The colour and style contrast strongly with the humble tone of samplers from most schools for the Poor.

Courtesy of St Clement Danes Primary School & Educational Foundation; St Clement Danes School (Chorleywood); and St Clement Danes School Charitable Foundation.

In the height of enthusiasm for Charity Schools, London accepted the challenge as if it were the beginning of a moral crusade. Ten thousand waifs and strays were snatched from warrens of filthy, cobbled, city streets. Charity children were scrubbed clean, fed, dressed in uniform, and housed in barracks like an army of reconstituted soldiers.

Once a year, the greatest orators of the established church called citizens to a celebrating sermon in St Paul's. Stands were erected on approaches to the cathedral, and ranks of cheering charity children greeted the parade who came to make donations to the worthy cause of rescuing the poor from sin. It was an awe-inspiring sight to those with glory in their eyes.

The tinge of fear that accompanies awe took a decade or two to show itself. People who were shocked by the spectacle slowly began to express their doubts in argument; and we may suppose the show hid a deal of embarrassing misjudgements. Would these child soldiers of a benevolent church grow to be an army of social revolution? The Civil War was within living memory.

SPCK schools were financed by the subscriptions of local gentry and Church of England congregations. The more they appeared to be recruiting agents for the doctrines of the established church, the more they seemed to be allied with Tory politics, and Jacobite apologists. Dissenters and Whigs withdrew their contributions. Books and pamphlets were printed against the Charity Schools, and their supporters were forced onto the defensive.

The Jacobite rebellion of 1715 sharpened these religious and political divisions. Defenders argued that good clothes issued to pupils would not breed vanity to rise in the world; for uniforms made the wearers visible objects of charity and reminded them continually of their servile rank. Founders began to dread that boys and girls in Charity Schools might be educated above the meanest offices in life.

Those who attacked Charity Schools conceded they had no opposition to Writing as such; they merely thought it iniquitous to be taught free. Writing was not necessary to moral instruction as Reading was; and to teach it might give the poor ideas above their station.

Furthermore it was work; the job of clerks in commerce, and a kind the gentry might want for their younger sons. Gentlemen got nothing by support of Charity Schools except the right to nominate scholars from the bright sons of acquaintances or employees. The desire to prevent the free teaching of Writing, and "inure the poor to labour", began to dominate the management of Charity Schools. Provision in them declined during the 18th Century: some closed; some became mean.

In this sad decline, samplers like Mary Windom's ceased to be made, and charity school girls were confined to the plain-sewing needlework that had been taught in parish and workhouse schools established in the days of the early Stuart Poor Laws. Then it had been possible to believe the "Poor" were individuals brought down by folly or the accidental disablement of sickness, age and mortality.

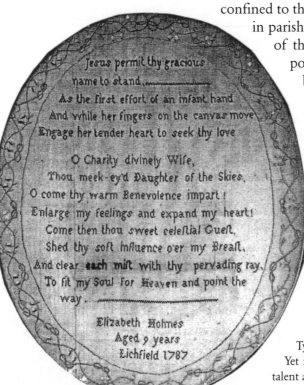

By 1800 the Poor were recognisable also as a class of people that bred more of their kind. Born poor, they remained poor, and were mostly without schooling of any sort. The more fortunate were strong, healthy and in employment; yet their wages did not rise to the cost of paying the fees that might have sent their children to school.

Girls afforded schooling by family income or charity aid, were taught to make Alphabet and Text samplers.

Text Sampler. Elizabeth Holmes, 1787.
Typical, in sombre black, of work from a Charity School. Yet its imaginative border, its sentiments and Elizabeth's talent at an early age, speak of care and dignity.

ALPHABET & TEXT SAMPLERS

The making of decorative samplers would have been a presumption too far for many girls at school. The Alphabet Sampler was more closely akin to useful needlework than to ornament. It required a small canvas, one stitch, and was usually confined to one or two colours at the most. Single Alphabets, cross-stitched, would be worked in capital letters. Many had a lower-case alphabet as well, and in more generous teaching the girls were taught to add numbers, punctuation marks and vowels. Only the strictest schools forbade the addition of the child's name and the date of completion. The more liberal would allow a few emblems, but the essential significance remained; the Alphabet Sampler was a preparation for the girls to offer their needlework as a qualification; to "mark" the linen of the gentry in whose homes they would find employment as servants.

Servants came in all conditions and ranks. Physicians were servants before they became professionals, and entered by side doors, not the front. Parish clergy fawned on their landed gentry. Live-in servants at large houses had their own hierarchies. A boot-boy or a maid between stairs was a long social distance from a butler or a governess. The most elevated were nevertheless servants and obliged to know it. Butlers did not marry into the families of their masters, but comely governesses could dream one day to catch the eye of a gentleman. They had more to fear from opportune rogues than hope from the love of honourable men.

Alphabet Samplers in all their variations show the ranks of society among less than affluent girls. Text Samplers were made neither by daughters of the gentry, nor by the general poor. Their status was somewhere between. Belief in the moral value of these exercises had as much to do with rigorous Protestantism as with social class.

Most were worked in school and made to hang in admonition on the wall rather than to be used as a certificate of skill. A simple text was sewn in stem-stitch letters. A passage was chosen from the bible, or a hymn; sometimes from another pious book such as "The Whole Duty of Man," the prescribed book of the Charity Schools. Generally the stitching was worked in simple black thread inside a sewn border. That too was plain rather than fancy, for the work was a serious commitment, not an indulgence. It was a reminder of the religious teaching of the school.

Private schools, catering for all the middling classes, were fond of samplers that helped the teaching of subjects other than needlework. Arithmetic tables and lists of history dates are rare, but survive to show that these unlovely samplers must have been made in many schools of their day. Samplers showing family chronology were perhaps made mostly in the home. Darning Samplers are extensions of school Needlework alone, and are described in a later chapter.

MAP SAMPLERS

Geography grew in popularity inspired by the three world voyages of Captain James Cook. His remarkable navigational feats sparked an interest in heavenly and terrestrial globes. It became fashionable for girls' schools to teach the making of Map Samplers. They began showing the terrestrial globe and the newly discovered continents. They are rare, for the needlework was demanding and the academic study fit only for imaginative minds.

The fashion for Map Samplers showing only England and Wales flourished in English schools during the Napoleonic Wars, either side of 1800. With great clarity they delineate the counties, and sometimes the county towns. Richer schools embellished the map samplers with little ships, boats, spouting whales and blowing winds. The certain purpose was that children should know the names of all the counties. These were learned by heart and catechised, as the rivers of the world were known in order of their length, and mountains in order of their height. Such was the infant subject of

Geography; and Needlework teachers seemed appropriate for that patient, painstaking learning.

Some Map Samplers were sewn over lines printed on the ground fabric or pricked out by a teacher. Where the shapes are awry, it is likely an adult copied the outlines freehand from an atlas.

Why some Map Samplers use British Ocean and others German Ocean for what we call the North Sea is an intriguing mystery. The Romans called it the German Ocean and so did Conan Doyle in the late 19th century. "Britain" was a national concept that began with the Stuart monarchy in the 17th century, and British Ocean is found in 1720. The Environmental Research Council still uses it. Heligoland was seized from Denmark in 1807, and in 1890 was ceded to Germany in exchange for Zanzibar. Map Samplers seem unaffected. The riddle may be solved when someone finds the atlases from which Needlework teachers copied their Counties of England and Wales.

Map samplers were often sewn without name or date. The custom may have come from the teacher's reluctance to acknowledge the work as their own, or from thinking something imposed on needlework was a less personal joy.

Map Sampler:
By H. Perry, the counties of England and Wales, a common form 1790 - 1820.

Girls in the meaner kind of private school sewed their samplers with crewel wool on rough canvas rather than silk thread on fine linen. Some examples are so poor, it is conceivable they may have been made in the most generous of Charity Schools, but at those dates few of them allowed the girls to make samplers of any sort, and if they taught sewing at all it was plain sewing.

Charity Schools came in all kinds; and great variation occurred in the teaching of girls. Yet the humble dullness that had settled on Poor School samplers was to last until sampler making itself was over. By doing plain sewing, hems, invisible mending, darning, and marking linen, they would have learned a valuable art. Girls took in work for subscribing families, and the money received helped pay for other studies. Such useful and recognised skills, opened a way to domestic service in the houses of the gentry.

The girls would have learned to make their letters in stitch so that they could mark the linen. In some places they would have learned all the crown-shapes that marked the ranks of the nobility, though the chance to use such a skill in noble houses would have been difficult to find. To show a certificate of these skills, many would have made an Alphabet Sampler. Sometimes called a "Marking" sampler, it was usually in a single colour, red or blue. Rarely an emblem or two was allowed, but modesty often demanded the child's identity was shown only by initials. A date would have been a presumption.

Such a sampler from those times is neither pictorial nor a piece of much literary attraction, but it is probably from a Charity School.

Distinguished among the Charity Schools were Foundling Hospitals or Orphanages. They boarded, clothed and fed the children, keeping them until they could be found a position to make them independent. To keep their long days occupied, more time was spent at their lessons than would have been afforded in a day school. Much of the girls' time was spent in plain sewing the infants' clothes, or other people's garments. But samplers were also made: Alphabet Samplers to show the talents needed in service; and Text Samplers - plain, black letters in a simple border.

The Text Sampler was a moral reminder for the child to keep when she left the care of the orphanage. It was meant to hang on the wall of her future garret, reminding her of friends, of the protection and strictures of her childhood, and of the debt she owed. The text reminded her of the trust due a benevolent God, or of his anger if she should offend. Too often they echo a piteous loneliness of a bleak life robbed of hope. Some reminded the girl of Jesus' sacrifice for the salvation of her soul. Very commonly it reminded her that the "Friends" who founded and ran the orphanage gave their time and cost out of Charity for the distressed.

Girls grow attached to their friends at school and a popular text listed the blessings of "Friendship" made at school.   The virtue of friendship was expressed in a riddle:

> *"Tell me thou knowing and discerning few*
> *Where I may find a friend both firm and true,*
> *Who dares stand by me in my deep distress*
> *And then her love and friendship most express.*
>
> Eleanor Watkins' sampler 1788. "

Eleanor's answer was "*my Mother!*" but it might be an aunt or anyone else to whom the sampler was addressed as a gift.

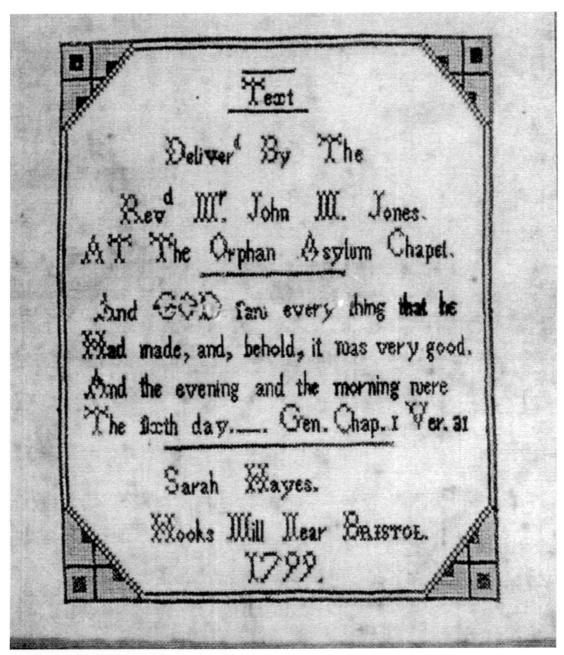

Sarah Hayes, Hook's Mill Orphanage, Bristol.
Actual size. Meticulous but small and modest.

In samplers made by the poor, the word "Friends" had the special meaning of those who paid for the girls' education, and the text was dictated by gratitude due. When an obligation of gratitude to "Friends" forms part of the text, it may have been made in a Charity School even if the name of the school is not given.

Quakers called themselves The Society of Friends, so for them Friendship would have the meaning of faith, mutual help, and consolation.

A Text Sampler by Mary Goffe 1791.
From an unknown Charity School.

Chapter 3
EMBLEMS OF CHARITY

"When constant Faith and holy Hope shall die,
One lost in certainty and one in joy
Then thou, more happy power, fair Charity,
Triumphant sister, greatest of the three,
Thy office and thy nature still the same,
Lasting thy lamp and unconsumed thy flame,
Shalt still survive!
Shalt stand before the throne of Heaven confest,
For ever blessing and for ever blest".

a late 18th C. sampler, name unknown.

Social mobility was slow and burdensome then. Many comfortable families feared Charity Schools actively promoted the triumph of merit, and that this would subvert the common people's proper respect for the gentry and civilization. Poor boys taught above their station were a danger to the nation; poor girls taught literacy were a danger to family stability. Persuasive books and pamphlets were written arguing that caution must check the reins of benevolence.

It was necessary for humble gratitude to condition the girls' expectations. Mean impulses dominated most Charity School samplers. The interests and affectations of richer children were generally excluded from the samplers of the poor. The manners proper to poverty were emphasised as much as religion.

In 1719 Captain Thomas Coram retired from a successful business in Boston and in the American colony of Massachusetts. In both places he had battled puritan prejudice against his Anglican faith. In London he was appalled to see dead and dying babies abandoned in the street, and he struggled against the contention that Foundling Hospitals only encouraged wantonness and prostitution.

The active support of George II's Queen Caroline led Coram to the aristocracies of power and fashion. In 1739 his persistent petitions succeeded in establishing a hospital "for the education and maintenance of exposed and deserted young children". In 1741 a grand new building costing £7,000 was erected on 56 acres of green fields near Great Ormond Street. Handel supported the charity with benefit performances and the artist William Hogarth gave enthusiastic help. The world of arts adopted the Foundling Hospital, and there, where before there had been no public place for exhibition, the Royal Academy was founded.

It was a remarkable achievement for one man. From Witney Antiques' catalogue, "Upstairs Downstairs, Plain & Fancy" we know someone sewed a text sampler in Foundling Hospital No 2. It was worked in hair on fine cotton and has no signature or initial. As they grew, the young orphan girls earned their keep by spinning and weaving cloth for service in the militia. A black boy rescued from slavery was taught Writing. The work of the girls has left no certain evidence.

In Bristol, the Little Red Maids had been walking happily in crocodile about the streets for many years before another Charity School for destitute girls was opened at Hook's Mills.

In 1801 Sarah Sennington, one of "The Blue Maids of Hook's Mills", left school to go into service. When she was ten years old in 1795, she had been the seventh child admitted to this *"ASYLUM FOR POOR ORPHAN GIRLS"*. Before she left school, she copied the purpose of the school on her sampler:

"The Design of this Institution is to rescue such real Objects of Compassion from the Contaminating Examples of Idleness and Vice, to instil into their tender minds the Principals of Religion and Morality, and to inure them to habits of Industry, and Cheerful Obedience, by Instructing and Employing them in every Kind of Household Work, which may Qualify them for Acceptable Servants in reputable places, And also in such Reading and Needle Work as may be useful unto them in any future situation in life. And if a Judgment may be formed from the general good order that prevails in the Asylum, and the obvious improvement in the children, there is every reason to hope that, with the blessing of Divine Providence upon the liberal exertions of the Patrons of so Beneficial an Institution, the greater part of those friendless and destitute females admitted into this house of refuge, will hereafter prove useful members of society, and an Ornament to CHRISTIANITY

Onto the work, she added the names of her Patroness, and the fifteen men on the Committee. But not her own.

The Industrial Revolution gathered the poor into crowded towns where there was work for the men but seldom schools for their children. Wages did not enable families to afford teaching at private schools. Dame Schools, which existed where the women went out to work, were little more than rough, child-minding rooms.

There were notable exceptions to this sparse provision for the schooling of the poor. Benevolent industrialists built estate houses for workers, looked after them in sickness and opened schools teaching their children to read, write and figure numbers. In the potteries, in cotton and wool mills and in the manufacture of chocolate or mustard, owners raised the expectations of their employees and the opportunities of the children. Many benevolent industrialists were influenced by Quaker ideals. Needlework and perhaps samplers may have been taught in their schools. But we must not look again for the kind of sampler from the poor that were met at St Clement Danes.

Schools of Industry.

During the eighteenth century Schools of Industry were set up for the poor. Guardianship was farmed out to overseers who expected to make a living from the work of the poor children, so they only taught manual labour or simple skills such as plaiting straw and spinning wool. There was no time or thought for reading and writing, and few would have taught needlework beyond the simplest repetitive sort. One at Cheltenham was restored as an orphanage under more generous impulses and with nobler patronage.

On 19th May 1806 Cheltenham Female Orphan Asylum School of Industry was instituted under the patronage of Queen Charlotte, the wife of George III. The aim was

"To clothe, maintain and educate female orphans and other female children of the poor. To inculcate into their tender minds such principles of religion and morality, to rescue them from the contamination of idleness and vice and train them up in the habit of industrious and cheerful obedience, by instructing them in such kinds of housework

as may qualify them for servants in respectable families."

The work girls did to help pay for their keep and clothing is shown below. It argues considerable skills and a dignity that few Workhouse Schools achieved. By no means could it have supplied the finance for the Cheltenham School. Charity subscriptions from the gentry around the town would have supplied the deficiency and kept their benevolent and private intentions alive.

A LIST OF THE PRICES FOR PLAIN WORK
Done at the Cheltenham Female Orphan Asylum & Old School of Industry.

	s	d.	to	s	d.		s	d.	to	s	
Fine Shirt .... fr.	1	6	:	2	6	Pinafore, with sleeves fr.	0	3	:	0	6
Ditto trimmed .... —	2	6	:	3	6	Muslin Handkerchief —	0	1	:	0	3
Shirt of inferior cloth —		8	:	1	6	Pocket ditto ...... —	0	½	:	0	1½
Boy's fine Shirt .... —		9	:	1	0	French Cambric ditto —	0	1½	:	0	2
Ditto trimmed .... —	1	0	:	1	8	Collar & pr. wristbands—	0	3	:	0	6
Ditto of inferior cloth —		6	:	1	0	Ditto, fine .... —	0	4	:	0	8
Fine Shift .... —		10	:	1	10	Coarse Sheets, per pr. —	0	8	:	1	0
Ditto trimmed .... —	2	0	:	2	3	Fine ditto .... —	1	0	:	1	4
Shift of inferior cloth —		7	:	1	0	Ditto of 3 breadths —	1	6	:	2	6
Night Shift ...... —	1	0	:	1	8	Pillow Cases, per pr. —	0	3	:	0	6
Ditto trimmed .... —	1	6	:	3	6	Table Cloth ...... —	0	2	:	1	0
Child's Shift ..... —		4	:	1	0	Towels, per dozen .. —	0	6	:	1	3
Night Cap, plain .. —		4	:	0	10	Dusters, per dozen.. —	0	4	:	0	8
Ditto, double borders —	1	0	:	1	6	Hemming, per yard —	0	½	:	0	1
Calico Dressing Gown —		6	:	2	0	Seaming, per yard .. —	0	½	:	0	1
Plain Petticoat .... —		6	:	0	10	Backstitching, per yd. —	0	¾	:	0	1½
Pockets, per pair .. —		4	:	0	8	Tucking, per yard .. —	0	½	:	0	1
Apron .... —		2	:	0	4	Marking, per letter —	0	¼	:	0	0½
Tippet .... —		2	:	0	6	Ditto, per figure .... —	0	¼	:		0
Pinafore......... —		2	:	0	5	Knitting, per ounce —	0	2	:		3

BABY LINEN.

	s	d.	to	s	d.		s	d.	to	s	d.
Shirt .... —	0	2	:		4	Plain Robe ...... —	0	8	:	1	6
Cap .... —	0	2	:		0	Bed Gown ...... —	0	6	:	1	0
Night Cap .... —	0	2	:		6	Petticoat .... —	0	6	:	1	0
Flannel .... —	0	3	:		0	Pinafore .... —	0	2	:	0	4

☞ *The charges between the limits will be regulated by the size and pattern of the work and the fineness of the materials.—It is requested that work sent may be CUT OUT with the GREATEST EXACTNESS, and a list be sent with it, also the name and residence of the person to whom the work belongs.—A bill will be given when the work is returned; and it is requested that the amount be paid at the time.*

An extra charge for work not cut out.

VOL. II.   D

A LIST OF PRICES FOR PLAIN WORK,
From their catalogue, "Diligence, Industry and Virtue". Courtesy of Witney Antiques.
The girls worked for their keep.

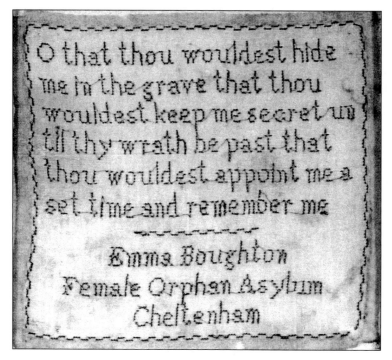

Emma Boughton c. 1790.
Actual size. Poverty and abandonment had all the weight of sin. Emma was taught to feel the wrath of God, and to plead there would be a place set for her in another life.

Schools of Industry, farmed out to efficient but unchristian keepers, brought them profit, but towns were still plagued by wild and disorderly children; and the manners and skills of their workhouse "education" did not fit them as servants in any respectable home. The stricter control of Cheltenham's new founders was as beneficial to the local gentry as it was to the poor and orphaned girls.

More! Though there was no promise that the children should be taught to read and write, the evidence of their samplers proves that they could read print letters with understanding, and write, though slowly, with their needles. Such work cannot have been done without calm, ordered and sympathetic guardianship.

However much the regime marked the poor girls into a permanent social category, it rescued them from unrestricted exploitation and degradation. The names of Charity Schools do not alone define whether their influences were kind or cruel.

The word "Charity" often eludes understanding, for it was extended to a variety of misfortunes. The boy who bullied young Oliver Twist was ashamed of his own uniform leather breeches and the taunts of "Charity!" that were hurled at him. The Bronte girls went to a Private Academy, but a boarding school that accepted the daughters of clergymen at reduced rates.

Even this much "Charity" left Charlotte with hatred at the loss of social status implied by the word, and she wrote in "Jane Eyre" of Charity as a stern and haughty guardian. Two sisters died at the school, giving her reason to condemn the regime without restraint. The samplers of the Bronte girls, on view in the Parsonage Museum, are typical of what might have been made at a good Poor School, but their dates show that they were done at home. In pious homes, Modesty in a girl was a becoming trait, and affectation foolish.

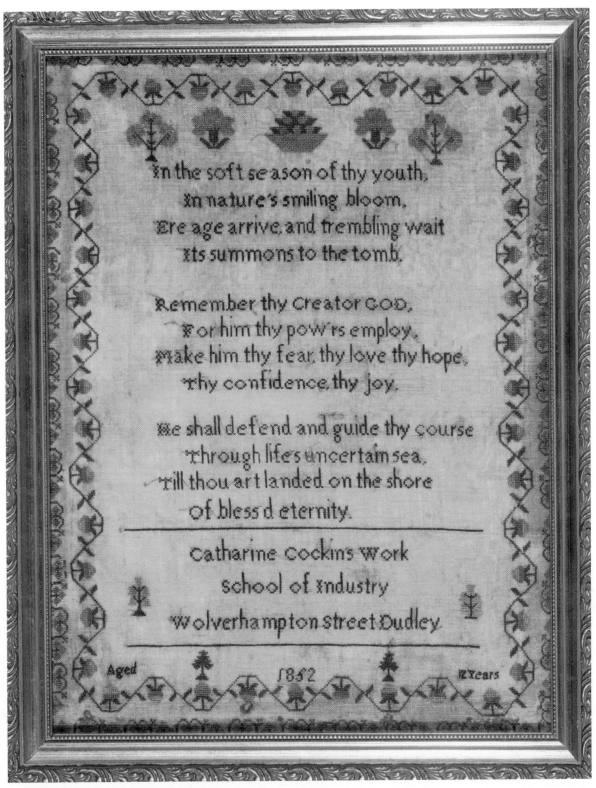

In the soft season of thy youth,
In nature's smiling bloom,
Ere age arrive, and trembling wait
Its summons to the tomb.

Remember thy creator GOD,
For him thy pow'rs employ,
Make him thy fear, thy love thy hope,
Thy confidence, thy joy.

He shall defend and guide thy course
Through lifes uncertain sea,
Till thou art landed on the shore
Of bless'd eternity.

Catharine Cockins work
school of Industry
wolverhampton street Dudley

Aged   1852   12 Years

Wolverhampton School of Industry. Catherine Cockin, 1852.
A Text Sampler embellished more generously than was commonly allowed in Poor Schools.

Orphanages and Charity Schools were not universally as drear as novelists found it convenient to depict. Some were indeed mean and insensitive, both to dreams of the future and nightmares of the present. But many aimed to raise the social hopes of diligent pupils, to give them personal dignity, and to make them literate as well as useful.

Good and bad schools were united in the belief that modesty and gratitude were the most becoming emotions of the poor. Politeness, industriousness and honesty were habits Charity Schools most encouraged. Idleness was the sin they most despised. Domestic service, and marriage to a good sturdy man was the kindest destiny they could imagine.

All the emotions and hopes that comfortable homes expected in their girls, were for the poor narrowed down to aspirations as thin as their samplers were plain. Poor girls also had puberty and the thoughts that went along with it: fear of death and damnation; hopes of salvation; the fortunes and dangers of love, of marriage, of a home and a family of ones own. All these were smothered by a philosophy reserved for the dependents of Charity. It was expressed in their samplers.

Ann Duggle's sampler made in 1820 at the Rochdale Free English School, generously pictures the school building, and two teachers along with other emblems. The text was however rather bleak.

> *"The Interest of the Poor and their Duties are the same, FOR;*
> *Cleanliness gives comfort;*
> *Sobriety brings health;*
> *Industry yields plenty;*
> *Honesty makes friends."*

The Bluecoat School in Hertford had been a Poor Charity School in the 17th century, but had risen in social and academic status to become almost a Private School. Its place was taken by the Greencoat School, whose clothes were in 1834 made by the girls of the Browncoat School, the Hartford School of Industry, a Poorest among Poor Schools. There, Mary Ann Bradding sewed on her sampler:

> *"The honour of a servant is her fidelity.*
> *Her best virtues are submission and obedience."*

Today, we shrink from confronting children with the limits of their independence. To encourage the notion of service in a child is laudable, but it seems unkind to form a servile mind. In true benevolence and charity, poor girls of the 18th century were fitted for the only decent career open to them. If this seems a poor endeavour, the life of poor women then was hard enough to forbid a sneer at the limited ambitions of their schools.

The worth of our purse, social status and political power were then more closely associated. The most learned divines taught that the gentry's morality toward each other was different from the duty they owed to the common people. Equality was a dangerous folly of the French Revolution. To deny the unequal station in which the rich and poor were cast, would have been perverse. It was sufficiently bold to allow that morality should ask them to live by the same rules.

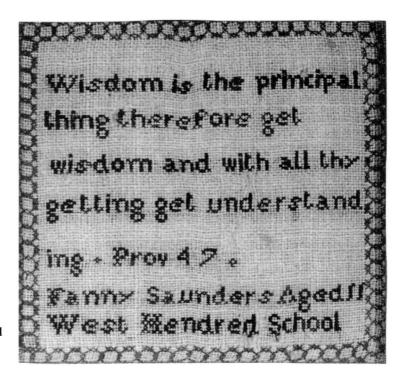

Fanny Saunders, West Hendred School. (9cm. sq.) Actual size.

Mary Ann Bradding, Hartford School of Industry.
Courtesy of Hertford Museum.

The unkindest facts of life may be expressed with love or with honest, if heartless, candour. Struggling to do the duty imposed on Charity School teachers, Mary Rayner's composed for her at a school in Ely, 1798, a universal epigram to be stitched under her plain Alphabet:

"COMPLAISANCE renders a superior amiable, an equal agreeable, and an inferior acceptable."

Fine needlework would not have made a proud girl acceptable in domestic service. Schools responded to economic facts. Some Charity Schools were, like the school at Ely perhaps, as warm and optimistic as the times allowed.

Condescension of the comfortably educated toward the poor was not universal. On rare occasions, respect for the minds of poor children saw through the habits and conditions of their poverty. Under her alphabet, Lucy Titchell in 1816 was taught to sew in her Charity sampler:

"The character of the person who commends you is to be considered before you set much value on the praise."
"To err is human, to forgive, divine."
"The wisdom consists in the regulation and government of the passions, not in a technical knowledge of arts and sciences."

To sew such sentiments, Lucy must have been spoken to with dignity and respect.

Humbleness reflected in Charity School samplers must not hide the fact that the girls who sewed them were among the more fortunate poor. The lives and prospects of those who never made samplers at all were often worse.

All this time the customs of affluent English families had settled on the sampler as an important element in the ritual of Childhood, and the verses that adorned them encouraged charity and sympathy toward the poor and distressed. The samplers of affluent families were greatly different from the samplers of the poor, but feelings proper to gentle up-bringing rehearsed what poor children should receive, and what so often they did not.

Chapter 4

THE EXAMPLE OF ACKWORTH

"DEEP
Humility is a strong Bul-
wark, and as we enter into it, we
find Safety and true Exaltation. The
Foolishness of God is wiser than Man, and
Being uncloathed of our own Wisdom, and
Knowing the Abasement of the Creature,
Therein we find that Power, to strive which
Gives to us Health and Vigour ---- The
Fear and Love of God begets Humility.

Anna Maria Laundy
Ackworth School
1792

One school stands out now, and stood out then, as an example of what Charity Schools could have been. Because we can identify the needlework samplers clearly, and because we know more of the individual girls who made them, we glimpse in their example a little of the lives of other poor sampler makers.

In 1758 the Yorkshire branch of Captain Coram's Foundling Hospitals was built in Ackworth. 2,644 abandoned babies were housed there before government grants ceased and the hospital was closed in 1773. The fine buildings were put up for sale, and bought by The Society of Friends.

The Society of Friends, or Quakers as they were called in derision, were a quiet and gentle people, distinguished by self-restraint, a strong call to duty, and a character of noble humility that made them very successful in business. By the second half of the 18th century, many Quakers had become wealthy, in banking, in brewing, and in other trades where usefulness, prudence and scrupulous honesty were recommendations.

But the Quakers also had poorer brethren; and though there were sufficient private Quaker schools for those who could afford the fees, the society felt for those who could not. Their children had to remain in ignorance or be contaminated by mixing with those of other faiths.

The Quakers borrowed £7,000 from the stock of their "Friends' School and Workhouse" at Clerkenwell. With this they purchased the buildings at Ackworth and in 1779 opened it for boys and girls "whose parents are not in affluent circumstances."

It is today a fine Public School that boasts a remarkable collection of its own samplers, made by pupils long ago. The collection testifies to patient teaching, and to the strict generosity of superintendents and visitors. It also shows the spiritual strength of Quakers, their concern for education, and their effective care of children in need.

Samplers were an important part of school life during the school's first sixty years. The school was then poised above abject poverty yet far from affluence, and may serve as an example of what life was like for others who made samplers in other schools. Some may have come from richer homes than the pupils of Ackworth, but not so many will have had more thought, competence and care given to their education. The samplers of Ackworth pierce a veil of years, which stands between our world and theirs.

Joseph Donbavand, a very able Writing-Master who taught the useful things well, was appointed as principal teacher. He stayed till 1817 during which time the most distinguished samplers were made; one by his own daughter. When full, the school housed about 300 pupils.

The children came from all corners of the kingdom, and generally stayed in Ackworth till the end of their schooling, when they were found occupations or returned to their parents. This complete separation from home was painful but not cruel. It was the choice that circumstance forced on conscientious poor parents, for travel was hazardous as well as expensive. The school was meant to shape the child with the same care and greater generosity than the parents could manage at home.

Like all schools, Ackworth was struck by epidemics of illness; and some children who went there never saw their parents again; the one dying in the school, the others in their far homes. Every churchyard in England shows that a sad number of those who reached school age, died in childhood. Such losses left room for love, grief and acceptance of reality. There were no vacations. Even for the more affluent in those days, private boarding schools advertised "absolutely no holidays," or restricted vacations to one a year, something introduced at Ackworth only in 1847.

Once a week, in winter or summer, the boys took a 6 a.m. leap into a chalybeate spring after a long, cold, half-mile walk from the school. It cleansed and invigorated the hardy, but cannot have been healthy for everybody. Their uniform leather breeches were changed in 1820 for corduroy.

The allowance of a pint a day of table beer was abolished in 1835. The girls had been allowed three quarters of a pint. The school provided a mantua maker, and the girls' uniform included these full cloaks. Girls were taught reading, writing and arithmetic like the boys, but in other ways their occupations were restricted. They shared some of the chores, but much of their time was given to the responsibility for making and mending the linen and the children's shirts and shifts. The needlework of the girls had gained such a reputation for excellence that they were able to take in outside work to raise money for the school.

The duties of the boys were more varied; they assisted at the cobbler's, the baker's, and in other workshops and gardens. In the proper season they helped gather the harvests from the school farm. The community attempted to be as self-supporting as possible.

Boys and girls met together only if they were related, when they could walk hand in hand in open view down the flagstones that led to the garden gates. A very inventive and elastic history of "cousins" grew up. The regime, like all good laws, was strict in the letter, but generous in the application.

The life of the children was conditioned by a sincere religious zeal shared with many other schools. Quakers did have their peculiarities. They had no set form to their religious meetings, nor were there ordained ministers. The congregation waited in expectant silence for those who felt the call to speak. The offerings of some Quakers were more refreshing than others, and they might sit where they could be best heard by all. Quakers expressed their equality before God, and their sense of community, by using the old second person, thee and thou, rather than the colder "you" into which the English language was slipping. They objected to the use of pagan names for days of the week or of months, so they spoke of Tuesday as "third day", and of August as "eighth month". They also had their own view of the proper means of discipline.

The seals of very many grammar schools set up in Tudor and Stuart times had included a picture of a master with a great birch of hazel twigs in his hand. The rod of correction stood as a more obvious symbol of education than the torch of light. It was believed that knowledge could only be got through pains, and that correction was best achieved by pain. Parents would have thought it very remiss of a teacher if their boys were not flogged for bad work and inattention, as well as for mischief. Short of that, there were of course other punishments.

Generally, girls were flogged less or not at all; but, in addition to the common dunce's cap and the punishment stool, the variety of punishments by humiliation was extensive. In another Charity School, girls used the letters they had learned on their samplers to make headbands with legends such as:- "LIAR" "DIRTY" or "I AM A THIEF" across the brow. Gentler examples of a common discipline were used in affluent homes and schools.

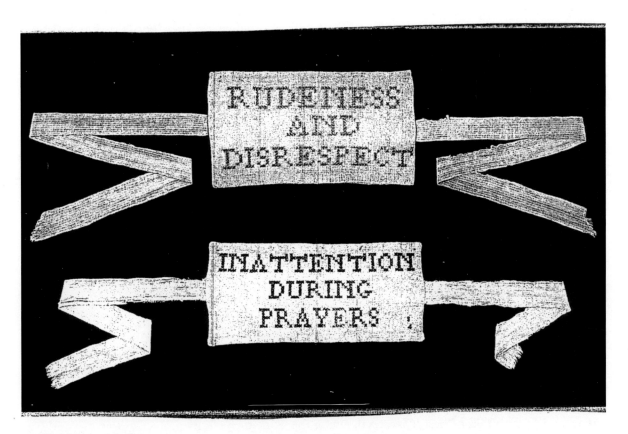

Punishment samplers.
From their catalogue, "Diligence, Industry and Virtue". Coutesy of Witney Antiques.
Gentle reprimands to be worn for shame. Perhaps from a nursery, possibly at Holkham Hall, Norfolk.

"Jane Eyre" tells of one girl standing on a stool wearing a badge of shame because she had made a blot in her copy-book. The rest of the class were encouraged to deride her, and this they did, fears and sympathies mingled in their hearts.

Elizabeth Clements had been a foundling at St Clement Danes, and in the absence of family name, she was, like Oliver Twist, given one by St Clements. Her sampler made in 1712 reflects a kind and confident regime. Made when she was ten years of age, one of its couplets was: *"This I have done, I thank my God, Without the correction of the rod."*

The rod was used at Ackworth; but with restraint, and under strict supervision. Other forms of punishment were administered without conscious intensity. The school retains a wooden token to be held by a child declaring it to be a punishment "For talking and being naughty". That was an indignity sensible for boys as well as girls, and effectively humbling without instilling fantasies of guilt or fear.

Ackworth provided itself with a penitential cell where rebellious children were locked until they had reached a state of repentance. If that seems harsh, consider what other response would control the brief but suicidal tantrums of despair orphans may have thrown.

The Quakers' sensitivity to the failings of all human beings, brought them to the forefront of the movements for penal reform and the protection of unguarded children. At Ackworth in 1830, forty-five years before it was made illegal, the use of climbing boys to clean the chimneys was forbidden.

Imagination has to flesh out these few facts to picture the girls in their bursts of fun and their moments of melancholy; the warm, bright summers and precious lazy intervals in scented fields; the drudgery borne with resignation; hunching shoulders in the goose-pimpled dawn ablutions; seated at their desks, quills tight gripped in chapped fingers; their food long-anticipated, and their meals monotonous; in their low hours, lying in the dark of a sleepless dormitory, crying quietly over some reprimand or slight; and in their tranquil, friendly moments, the chores done, sitting by a chosen companion and speaking out their secret thoughts while fingers and eyes concentrated on finishing a letter in their sampler.

Imagine the great stone building of the school, the grounds before it speckled with children, moving sedately or skipping blithely. Hear the sharp voices, lively or sad, angry or kind, splintering the silence that stands between us.

School-life was harsher for many other little sampler-makers; and the samplers made at Ackworth in its early days had an extraordinary quality. Three kinds were made regularly, and another by choice; all restricted to three subdued colours. Girls must have practised their letters on small pieces of cloth before beginning their first.

Lettering Samplers

Early in their lessons, girls made a lettering sampler, either in black, or red silk; sometimes in a mixture of both. They were sewn inside a rectangular or oval border. There seems to have been choice in the shape of the rectangle, and which way up the oval hung. The contents within the border are evenly balanced in conformity to the outline, and planning must have been most exact. Probably there were differing examples already made for the girls to copy. The weave of the cloth was close, and the lettering done with the smallest cross-stitch, giving the work great clarity.

The name of the school and of the child, and a date, always appear. Then came a line of numbers and alphabets in large and small letters. With these, is a line of diphthongs and punctuation marks, and the conjoined letters (ligatures) printers then used in cases where s, c or f, were attached to the following letter. There is a short additional text. These features were copied from Donbavand's Copy Sheets; and when found in lettering samplers show they exemplified work being done with the pen and not Reading alone. The texts are well punctuated and spelt; the alphabets used, even in the earliest known in 1785, are Joseph Donbavand's full 26 letters.

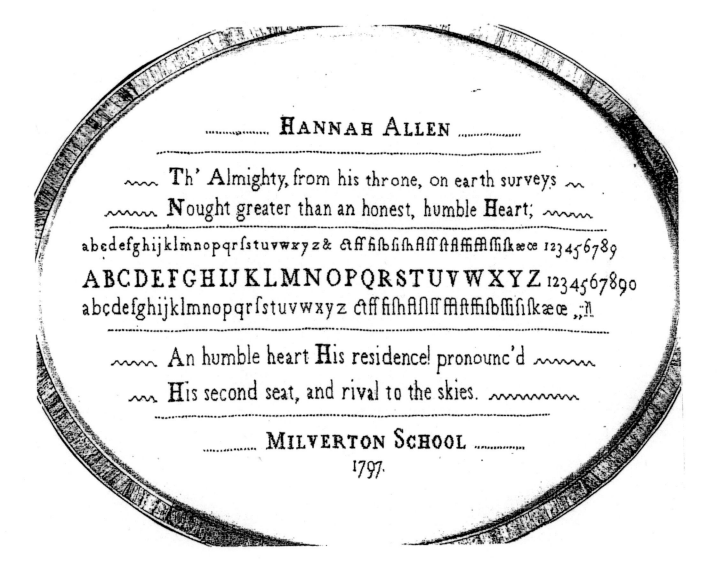

Hannah Allen 1797.
Milverton was a Quaker School that copied the Lettering and Darning Samplers of Ackworth. Their samplers typified lessons designed to fit girls for useful and remunerative skills. Poverty was a matter of regret, not shame, and Quaker Schools taught children how to escape it by their own efforts and talents. They preferred competence and plain speaking to fanciful arts.

About 1808, red appeared in the black work. Sophisticated lettering conjunctions were abandoned, and within the next years the text passage disappeared to make a simpler alphabet sampler.

RESIGNATION.

Since all the downward tracts of time
  God's watchful eye surveys,
Oh! who so wise to choose our lot
  And regulate our ways.

Since none can doubt his equal love,
  Unmeasurably kind,
To his unerring gracious will,
  Be every wish resigned.

Good when he gives, supremely good,
  Nor less when he denies,
Even crosses from his sovereign hand,
  Are blessings in disguise.

M. A. Hunton, Ackworth School.

1829.

An Ackworth Text Sampler. M.A Hunton, 1829. In December 2006, Carol Humphrey's new book, "Quaker School Girl Samplers from Ackworth" ISBN 0-9552086-1-0, will be published by 'Needleprint'. This thorough description of a remarkable collection will make its history available to all for the first time.

Text Samplers

The text samplers, which all girls made, were sewn within plain borders that were often mitred at the corners. The name of the school and child, along with the date were sewn. The texts were composed in the same precise lettering, and were chosen from an anthology appropriate to their faith:

"The Duty of Man" (*Transient is human Life, all Flesh is Grass*) : "Virtue" : "Deep Humility" : "Solitude" : "Human Frailty" : "One" (*charity*) : "When" (*thou considerest thy wants*) : "An Evening Thought" : "On Providence" (*God works in a mysterious way, His wonders to perform*) - this is a well known hymn, but not found elsewhere in samplers.

A school favourite already illustrated, called "Resignation", was worked by Susanna Wright in 1822. It was popular in samplers made at other schools.

A noticeable feature of Ackworth samplers is that the alphabets and texts have been given plenty of room, and placed carefully in a blank sheet just as the offerings at worship were dropped into a waiting silence. The obsessive concern for economy in most charity schools is absent, and the confident generosity of design in Ackworth samplers contrasts strongly with some others.

Emma Topham, 1837. Copyright Ackworth School Estates.
An Ackworth Alphabet Sampler, supplanting the earlier Lettering Sampler before Needlework was abandoned to make room for academic lessons. Emma was not a registered scholar and her sampler which may have come from the village, suggests that Ackworth co-operated with local schools.

An Ackworth Darning Sampler, Ann Trump, 1797.
Ann made her first darning sampler in 1794, a set of plain white-work darns kept at the school. This was made with contrasting colours to show the intricacy of damask darns. Its present whereabouts is unknown.

A contrasting, decorative Darning Sampler from an unknown, private, school. Many were anonymous, as this, typical of those made by daughters of gentle families.

Darning Samplers

Following those early samplers, girls were allowed to begin a darning sampler in their spare time, and by choice. Again, name and school appear and a date. These were surrounded by eight plain and damask darns done in two colours to show the crossing stitches. Later darning samplers had fewer darns, and the name of the school might be missing. If these or any Ackworth samplers are turned over, the quality of the needlework becomes more apparent. Every stitch is reversed on the back, and every letter or design has been tidied off, with no trailing threads or joins to adjacent works. They can be read cleanly front and back. That is a feature of 17th century samplers and will be found rarely later on. It is invariable in an Ackworth sampler until at least 1837.

Medallion Samplers

In their final year at school, some pupils were making their principal sampler. It did not invariably include the name of the school, but its tradition is so distinctive that it is instantly recognisable. Each is unique, but all are made from a corpus of emblems and designs peculiar to Ackworth. The rectangular border is made of touching halved octagons, in which geometric designs and formalised flowers are sewn. The centre is spread with whole octagons, or wreathed floral ovals. The spaces inside these may be used for a name, or for the school, but most show one of the many Ackworth emblems that assist identification.

Ackworth's Medallion Sampler; M. Dickinson, 1798,
Sewn in olive green and black. The style and emblems are distinctive of the school, and of a single instructress. E.D. would probably be the initials of a parent to whom the work was dedicated.

Ackworth emblems included a circlet of rose-buds; a squirrel in a tree; a convolvulus; a passion flower; a bird on a branch; or two facing each other, one holding out a twig to the other; a posy holder shaped like a horn in which a tulip and a carnation can be recognised among other flowers. Most distinctive of all is a swan sailing by reeds under a tree. The sky sometimes holds a small flock of birds.

Swans are full of grace, and wear the white of purity. They are birds faithful to death in their mating. But perhaps the designer of this emblem was thinking of the way the pen rides her cygnets on her back, and how the little ones sail safely across the water, snug between the protection of her great wings. Dealers sometimes call these, "swan samplers", without recognising from whence they came. That is a pity.

The rest of the sampler is used to fill out family initials, or perhaps the initials of friends. Often the spaces are used to sew an alphabet, but if so, the letters are scattered all over the sampler. Finally comes the dedication. When this appears, it may say, "Tho absent yet not forgot"; more commonly, "A Token of Love". These samplers were made as gifts.

The girls used similar designs for gifts of pin-cushions and purses. In a letter home, one girl begged coloured silks or ribbons to make such things gay. A pin-cushion made in 1790 shows the two birds facing each other.

A Pin Cushion made at Ackworth as a present.
Copyright Ackworth School Estates.

Ackworth emblems are not taken from heathen mythology, nor from the occult fancies of the emblem books. They come from natural observation. Here, it is the emblem of a loving gift in the courtship of rooks; the searcher gravely passing the precious product of his labours to the builder?

An institution is not a home, and it is worth remembering that the lives of poor and orphan girls elsewhere were mostly hard and uncertain. Yet hardship and uncertainty are not necessarily the outcome of poverty alone. They were often inseparable from being born to a struggling adventure such as the colonisation of America. Early American samplers are as simple and plain as the lives from which they sprang, and Ackworth School was to have a decided impact on their traditions.

AMERICAN SAMPLERS

Two samplers attributed to the generations of the Pilgrim Fathers are not perhaps typical. Land in the American colonies was good, but it had to be cut out of the wilderness before life was anything but hard and dangerous. From the outset, the democratic nature of the settlements and the puritan zeal of its religion urged parish schools upon the people, so that children could learn to read their Bibles. The girls' samplers were most often plain Alphabet Samplers such as we should expect from poorer homes in England. As the dangers of the native Indians retreated westward, there was time for a few emblems and flowers to adorn the alphabets and verses.

Poverty comes in many guises. The pioneers of the American West had many discomforts and often went short of food. The dangers of their sea passage from tempests, and from hostile natives on land, required hardihood and determination. The privations of their life exposed them to hurts and diseases that wiped out families. They were poor in every comfort, convenience and necessity; but they were not poor in spirit. Hope had not died in their hearts as it had in the homes of so many of the poor of Europe.

The poem of dedication on the Statue of Liberty reads:

"Give me your tired, your poor,

Your huddled masses yearning to breathe free,

The wretched refuse of your teeming shore,

Send them, the homeless, tempest tost to me."

The women who came sewed and mended clothing, and the girls made samplers. One does not hang embroidery in a sod hut or on the walls of a log-cabin. Their alphabet and text samplers told simply their respect for learning and the importance that everyone should read and write. Modest though they may seem today, many Frontier American samplers are as good an example of their spirit as the Kentucky rifle was of their peril.

Those who pushed the frontiers into lands that had to be won and made safe came from many countries, with the languages and customs of other nations than England. In American samplers can be found the influences of German, Dutch, and Scandinavian traditions mixed with the home grown-traditions of their new world.

Before the revolutionary wars, the eastern states of America had engendered their own industries and their own leisured gentry. In rich schools, girls made pictorial samplers like those of rich English families, but with a style peculiarly American. Instead of a thin border garland, the girls sewed a frame, wide enough to hold its own pictures and emblems. As a sign that the girls were taught pen-writing at school, their alphabets included cursive letters much earlier than they did in England.

In the 1790's Ackworth received a visit from leaders of a school at Westtown, Philadelphia, a school founded and inspired by the success of Ackworth. With them came a Needlework teacher, Rebecca Jones. She returned to America with the text sampler of Candia Power, an Ackworth pupil, whose sampler was sewn on woollen cloth. Samplers were also made on linen and tiffany gauze. The full range of Ackworth Samplers, with minor adaptations, was then made at Westtown, and the school has now a collection of nearly a hundred of them. The example and influence spread to other Quaker schools opened in Virginia, Delaware, New Jersey, New York, and Massachusetts.

Jane Merritt's New York sampler, dated from "Boarding School, Nine Partners, 9th Month. 16th. 1803", shows half octagons, and five of the central emblems of Ackworth.

In Westtown, sewing was the only subject offered that really differentiated the curriculum of the girls from that of the boys; but in 1843 needlework ended, to be replaced by academic subjects, including the classics. The boarding school had inspired richer families to patronise it, and something similar was happening in England.

In 1785 a boarding school was established in York by Esther and William Tuke who had been instrumental in founding Ackworth. Its object was the "Education of FRIENDS CHILDREN in general, especially Girls, consistent with the Principles we profess ..... and ..... the advantages of ACKWORTH SCHOOL, and desirous that a similar opportunity of a guarded Education may be extended to such girls, who, by reason of their Age, or on account of the circumstances of their Parents or Friends, are not sent thither."

By 1830, Quakers poor enough to require a charity school became fewer as the prospects for each generation were raised. At the same time, the reputation of Ackworth encouraged prosperous Quakers to let their daughters finish their education there. The requirements of a full liberal education began to diminish the importance of needlework.

In America the influence of Westtown needlework had spread. In 1823 Sarah Ann Hartman sewed a sampler that contained some of the old Ackworth emblems. Sarah's New Jersey school must have been for private pupils because it is as colourful and elaborate as any made at home; but among the verses and other emblems are found two of the octagons, the squirrel, the rose garland, the bird in the tree, the posy holder with a carnation, and the swan with its rushes and overhanging tree. This sampler has a border of a vine with convolvulus and roses entwined, which is similar to one developed at Westtown. This design, and an alien rooster, is shared by Martha C. Hooton's work of 1827. No doubt they went to the same school. In her sampler the posy holder is further decayed, and the swan has lost her tree and reeds, but faint though they are, the echoes remain of a contact with Ackworth forty years earlier.

Other Quaker Schools

Beating a path to the doors of Ackworth, other English Quaker schools copied its better sampler patterns. South Brent School had the emblems and style exactly enough.

In the 19th century, studious girls in many schools were used as monitors to teach younger children. They were paid a very small salary, but began an apprenticeship to become Pupil-Teachers. The most distinguished of these left their home school to begin a teaching career. The patterns within needlework teaching were not dictated by text-books but by the personal accumulation of examples. Just the same collection of personal examples was used in Writing and Mathematics copybooks. The skills and patterns of Donbavand's alphabets, and the mistress's samplers, moved from Ackworth as girls moved on as teachers to other schools.

Wigton Friends' School was begun in 1815. In 1816 Hannah Beeby's sampler showed Ackworth's Medallions incorporated with Donbavand's lettering (with the long and short s) and the name of the school. Jane Graham in 1819 sewed a plainer lettering sampler.

Milverton, in Somerset, boarded pupils until they were sixteen, for £35 a year. Their Alphabet and Darning samplers were similar to those at Ackworth, though the octagons do not appear. Girls made Map Samplers to show their studies included Geography.

Sidcot School, also a fee-paying Quaker school, was founded in 1808 and leaned upon the experience of Ackworth. In the 1820's its Darning Samplers show the influence.

No other school had an influence on samplers quite like Ackworth's, and perhaps no other faith was as successful as the Quakers' in adapting to the dignity of poor children, studies that had begun in royal courts.

One school, so far unidentified, left behind samplers whose letters are mostly made of four-sided black stitches. That simple dull colour seems to mark them out as coming from a Charity School, yet the inscriptions are heavily drawn from Roman and Greek history, the curriculum of a typical Boys' Grammar School. They are strikingly distinctive, and come from the middle of the nineteenth century, when a combination of poor, classically taught, female pupils must have been a rare thing.

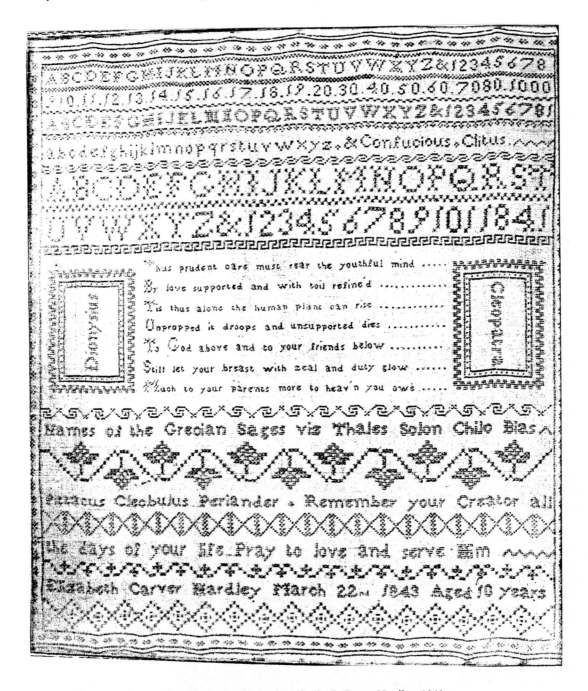

Another distinctive but unidentified School sampler. Elizabeth Carver Hardley, 1843.

At this time a surprising number of ancient Poor Schools were undergoing a metamorphosis into Public Schools. It happened to the "Red Maids School" in Bristol. During a disastrous period of frequent staff changes, serious indiscipline became common. Between expulsions and parents withdrawing children in protest, the city fathers were harassed by complaints. There were epidemics of fever and smallpox. Diseases such as "itch" (Scabies) and Ringworm were rife and arose from poor hygiene. It was a time when day schools for the poor suffered the same common difficulties, which were consequences of poverty at home, not just at this boarding school. By the 1870's, in spite of improvements to the teaching, there were complaints that "£3000 was spent just for the sake of supplying Clifton people with servants."

The public was saved expense while the school got a better reputation by opening to fee-paying pupils from responsible families wanting an academic education.

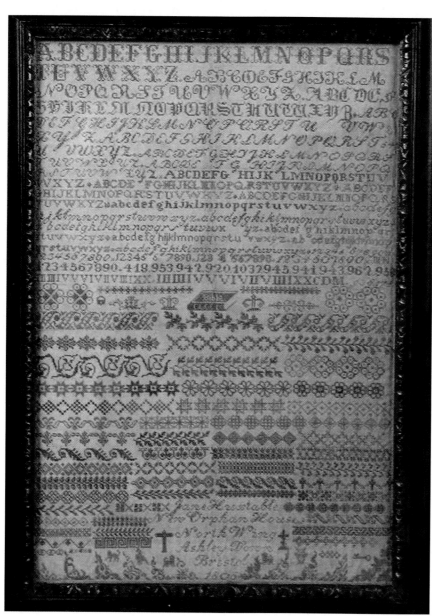

Traditional Sampler from a Bristol Orphanage. Jane Huxtable. 1805.

The date has been altered. George Muller opened his first Bristol orphanage in 1832 and this style of sampler comes much later. Jane was born in 1850 and left the orphanage to become a servant soon after making her sampler at the age of 15 in 1865.

Courtesy of a private collection by Pam Hall, Watford, who has discovered more about Jane and her family.

By the turn of the century, the spread of elementary schools allowed the Red Maids to become a "Higher Grade School", i.e. one teaching secondary subjects.   The change was wholly successful, though it no longer answered its original purpose.

Sympathy for poor children oscillated between extreme views; that they were innocent "Little Red Riding Hoods" or, every one of them, coarse and irremediably wayward. The characters, needs and potentials of the poor are as varied as the rich, but poverty often leaves indelible marks. Free day-schools, new orphanages, and new opportunities for employment, hesitatingly, lessened that stamp on the childhood of the poor.

Very late, and briefly, one group of Poor Schools produced samplers recognisably their own. From one of the two Bristol Charity Schools already mentioned had come samplers of the humble sort then expected, and it may be supposed that they were the culmination of a curriculum of plain-sewing needlework described in Chapter 7. In the late 1860's, when the fashion for elaborate samplers was dying out in homes and schools, the New Orphan House, at Ashley Down, Bristol produced large and intricate samplers sewn with red cotton thread on white cotton cloth.

Ashley Down was one of five orphanages founded by George Muller, the German minister of an independent church in the town. By 1870 the schools housed over 2000 destitute orphans. It is amazing that one town could produce so many, but cholera, tuberculosis and other diseases abounded, and records show how often mother and father perished in the same epidemic. All Muller orphanages produced samplers based on tightly packed, distinctive alphabets; rows of continuous patterns; and motifs peculiar to the needlework of the homes. They are meticulous more than individual; a small bible figures in the centre of most, and a slight degree of choice is limited to arrangement of the elements. Many of these samplers named the school, the pupil, and sometimes the teacher or, poignantly, the child's admission number. Later examples included a short text.

From the memories of orphans, we are told that the children were not instructed, but learned the patterns from each other. People who know and love samplers do not underestimate the talents of children; but those memories must be incomplete. There needed to be painstaking instruction. The children probably remembered making the Bible emblem, or a rocking horse, or one of the typical triangular patterns, while sitting by an older child and copying her work. Copy was how children learned to write, and copy was how the first samplers were made. But it was the teacher that dominated the quality of needlework, as it does of every subject in schools today.

One of the Ashley Down orphans became the first lady Mayoress of Bristol, a tribute to its remarkable success with disadvantaged children.

A tradition of excellence in a school, whether in academic work, in art, music, drama, athletics, or samplers, is an influence that gives dignity to all its pupils. To be any good, a school must do at least one thing really well.

A School Sampler 1804; Elizabeth Bancroft.
Variety of stitch; "nota bene"; initials, of family or school friends; early use of script letters; 26 letter alphabet and good punctuation; careful yet sombre needlework. Perhaps from a school of sturdy self-help and religious independence?

A sampler of the unpretentious but not destitute poor.
Margaret Putman was probably a day pupil at a British or National Society Voluntary Poor Schools teaching all who could not afford private fees. The stitches, darns and button-holes are from a plain-sewing curriculum. Made at Standard 5, a system probably dating it c. 1870 - 80.

Chapter 5

THE RICH TRADITIONS OF ENGLISH SAMPLERS.

"The world is a sity and full of streets
Death is a market where all men must meet
If breath was a thing that money could buy
The rich they would live and the poor only die
But god in his wisdom hath ordered it so
That the rich and the poor together must go."

c.1711, anonymous but dedicated to Anne Hunt.

Needlework was a necessity: embroidery was an art. Any complicated idea for improvement or innovation had to be tried out first on spare cloth. Failures would be unpicked, but the most successful motifs were kept to be copied onto the embroidery and to remain as an example if it was needed again. That spare trial cloth was a Sampler. Adult samplers had no end; they grew throughout a needlewoman's life, rolled up in the workbox and passed around the sewing circle to inspire emulation and to give encouragement.

Some time during the reign of Elizabeth a new purpose began to make the samplers of children more like a single rite of passage than a continuing collection of good examples. It was more than an introduction to reading, though that was the origin of the tradition that young girls should sew an alphabet into their work. By 1660 a pattern of beginning, completing and ending a single task had been established

It was in affluent homes that the most generous traditions of those Needlework Samplers were formed. Though the needs, fears and hopes of poor children are not altogether different from those of more fortunate families, what poor children received was a humble and restricted imitation of those purposes and forms. Understanding the samplers of the poor is incomplete without knowing the traditions of affluent families who made needlework samplers an important ritual in the childhood of their daughters.

For poor girls with any pride or ambition, it was these traditions they wished to follow.

Many things conspired to make the traditions of English samplers different from other European countries. The Protestant Reformation, and its peculiar English outcome, shaped the symbols that were commonly embroidered on the children's work. The earliest known European sampler dates from about 1550, and shows the familiar icons of the Catholic faith; the emblems of the Cross; hammer, pincers, nails, ladder, spear, sponge, chequer-board, seamless robe; and the cockerel that called Peter three times to deny Christ.

All these, and IHS, the consonants of Jesus' name, the flaming and bleeding sacred heart, and other religious symbols were anathema to the Protestants who rooted out what they considered idolatrous or superstitious images. They were hacked or washed out from the reformed churches and were not tolerated in printed books or in the customs of Protestant households.

The earliest English sampler to survive was made at the end of the Tudor period. It is already more a childish delight than a work-piece, though it was probably sewn by a young servant of the family. Covered with symbolic emblems, it contains none of those that had been the common icons of Catholic Europe. Two and a half centuries followed during which the emblems of English childhood samplers formed their own traditions.

Catholic symbols, such as crucifixes and the instruments of the cross, would not have been openly acceptable after the reign of Mary Tudor. They reappear, infrequently, on samplers at the approach to Catholic emancipation in the reign of George IV.

Emblems

Sixteenth century art made great use of emblems; symbolic images that told of mystical connections between an object and its potent message. Emblem books were printed so that the messages of common emblems could be interpreted. Similar pictorial messages dotted the samplers made by children. The flowers and fruits they sewed often decorated samplers with emblematic significance. The carnation was obliquely, holy blood; the acorn spoke of a moral potential in young things. The mother-bird on a nest of pelicans was thought to tear her breast and feed her young with blood; an allegory of Christ more subtle than the Crucifix.

A garland of honeysuckle, trees, domestic pets, ships or little houses might or might not have an implied message. Mermaids appeared in samplers without any obvious religious significance. Distrust of feminine beauty formed a strong element in the education of girls, and might have been intended by it; but it is probable many emblems were liked and copied, without concern for their exact meaning. Plants and creatures that adorned domestic embroidery were as often sewn on samplers with no other significance than the delight they gave. Motifs do not have to be emblems.

In place of overt Catholic symbols, English embroideries used images from the Old Testament; moral symbols and pictures familiar to domestic life among country gentlemen. A popular moral story was pictured as an icon of Adam and Eve, with a serpent in the tree. It was a parable about the sin of disobedience; and as the sampler became more and more a child's completed task, the emblem spoke of a child's obedience to parents, and to all authority sanctioned by God and the Bible.

By 1700 adult pictorial needlework associated the Old Testament patriarchs with reverence for the monarchy. In a landscape, Solomon and Sheba appear clothed but slightly different from Charles II and Catherine of Braganza. A principal structure, common to the needlework of the time, was a tall, royal tent or pavilion with a notched fringe about its head. In medieval days when royalty had no settled home to depict, and went on progression or campaign about the kingdom, these campaign tents were familiar in painting. The symbol spoke equally of English or Old Testament royalty.

If the principal figures in the embroidery are not clear from the emblems that surround them, they may be identified by popular bible stories. Abraham's readiness to sacrifice Isaac, appeared in adult embroideries as a powerful moral story about the Jews' abandonment of human sacrifice. The depiction of a patriarch, a woman and a child before a tent seldom represents Abraham, Sarah and Isaac.

Women at their needlework were more sympathetic to the story of Abraham dismissing Hagar and Ishmael to the wilderness. Women were often at the whim of men, and it was a comfort to be sure of God's watchful eye over the pious and humble. They felt for Hagar who left her son in the shade of a bush because she could not bear to see him die of thirst. They rejoiced in God's deliverance of both.

If pictures were beyond the skill of a girl at her sampler, reverence for royal authority could be shown by a royal monogram. Rejection of the Commonwealth's attempts at social levelling, and restoration of respect for the nobility is implied by a row of varied crowns among the emblems of samplers. Under each was often an initial signifying the rank of chivalry. To place Queen and King in the centre a 19th century order was: B (baron); Bt (baronet); E (earl); D (duke); Q ; K ; P (prince); L (lord); M (marquis); V (viscount); and P.

The last P must have been Princess. Wouldn't you know she came last?

If a C appears, that would be Count, a European rather than English title.

From a Scottish Sampler, c.1720.
Ranks of the nobility shown in eight crowns. From "Samplers and Tapestry Embroideries," M. B. Huish, 1913.

By the middle of the eighteenth century, embroidery was no longer the perquisite of nobility and the gentry. It was the pride of ladies from the emergent middle-classes.

Catholic symbols on a French sampler.
Emblems of the crucifixion, the instruments; ladder, nails, hammer, pincers, spear, seamless robe, chequerboard, and the cock that crowed.

Chapman's Motifs ('slips') on plain silk as for sale.

The Chapman's Motifs

When Charles II was restored to his father's throne the fashion for embroidery seems to have taken on a new delight. Tapestries and furnishings, panels and samplers, survive in a quantity that so far outstrips the survivals of earlier times, that royal enthusiasm seems to have boosted the fashion. A delight in embroidery increased the use of samplers by young girls and affected the kind of things that they sewed.

Haberdashers and travelling chapmen were by now selling emblems and motifs already made up on a plain silken or linen ground. These "slips" were cut out and applied with stitching to the scene needlewomen were sewing for their stump-work panels and furnishings, elevating the design with a professional skill the ladies might not have accomplished without help. Couchant stags, clown-faced lions, carnation sprays, caterpillars and royal figures were stock embroideries, and became so familiar they were copied in simpler stitches onto Children's samplers. Since many of these motifs originated in the pattern books of the previous century, it is not surprising to find their images repeating themselves, in adult works and juvenile samplers, throughout the country.

Chapman's Motifs rescued from a decayed 17th C. domestic embroidery.

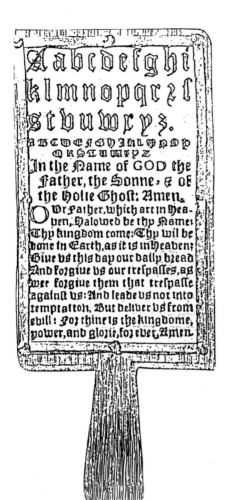

A Horn Book. c. 1600.

Essential instruments for children to learn reading, the backs of horn books provided a convenient bat to strike a feather-flighted ball in a game of "battledore & shuttlecock". By 1800, the wooden bat was replaced by a cardboard battledore and the sport had grown into the adult game of badminton.

The Alphabet

Horn-books were familiar tools to teach children their ABC and the beginnings of reading. A transparent sheet of horn was fixed over a printed paper that began with the letters of the Alphabet in upper and lower case letters. They were often followed by easy syllables and a short moral sentence. A copy of it became the introduction to most samplers. Soon it became traditional to include the new Arabic numbers, associating a child's early lessons, with the numbering of Biblical verses. Common throughout Europe, alphabets and numbers are not distinctive of English samplers. In France the alphabet so predominated that samplers are called almost contemptuously, "A-Be-Ce-De's".

"An help to Children to learn to read Eng-lish."
From A BOOK FOR BOYS AND GIRLS, OR Country Rhimes for Children, 1686, by John Bunyan. This was Bunyan's Horn-book page.

An help to Chil-dren to learn to read Eng-lish.

In or-der to the at-tain-ing of which, they must first be taught the Let-ters, which be these that fol low.

A B C D E F G H I K L M N O P Q R S T V W.

a b c d e f g h i k l m n o p q r s t u w x y z.
A B C D E F G H I K L M N O P Q R S T V W X Y Z.

a b c d e f g h i k l m n o p q r s t v u w x y z.
A B C D E F G H I K L M N O P Q R S T V W X Y Z

a b c d e f g h i k l m n o p q r s t v u w x y z

The Vowels are these, a, e, i, o, u.

As there are vow-els, so are there Con-so-nants, and they are these.

b c d f g h k l m n p q r s t v w x y z.

There are also dou-ble Let-ters, and they are these.

ct ff si ssi fl fi ffi st sh.

Af-ter these are known, then set your Child to spel-ling, Thus T-o, to. T-h-e, the, O-r, or, I f, if I-n, in, M e, me, y-o-u, you; f-i-n-d, find, S-i-n, sin : In C-h-ri-s-t, Christ, i-s, is, R-i-g-h-t-e-o u-s-n-e-ss, Righ-te-ous-ness.

And ob-serve that e-ve-ry word or syl-la-ble (tho ne-ver so small) must have one vow-el or more right-ly pla ced in it.

For instances, These are no words nor Syl-la-bles, be-cause they have no vow-els in them, name-ly, fl, gld, strght, spll, drll, fll.

Words made of two Letters are these, and such-like, If, it, is, so, do, we, see, he, is, in, my.

Words con-sist-ing of three Letters,

But, for, her, she, did, doe, all, his, way, you, may, say, nay.

In the sixteenth century, printed books had dropped a couple of Anglo-Saxon sounds from their fonts, replacing them with gh and th. Books added the English W, and Greek characters X, Y, and Z to the old Latin alphabets. Y was used instead of th for a while but pronounced with the hard sound of "the" and "that", not the ye that was a version of you. Y retained both vowel and consonant uses. In early alphabets I stood for J with the soft sound of the Dutch Jan or Scots Ian. To give it a harder sound, an H was added; i.e. Jhon, later John.   By the time it could sound as in jam, it had ceased to be a vowel.

Sampler alphabets began with the 24 letters of copybooks. U and J were sewn into sampler verses for many years before they found their way into school alphabets. 26 letter alphabets are rare before 1780, unusual before 1800; after 1820 they may be expected. In the middle period, varieties of 24, 25 and 26 letter alphabets show the transition.   Part of that transition was the dropping of the old, long variation of an S. It continued in writing for a generation after it disappeared from printed books and samplers.

The letters were often sewn in pairs of capitals and pairs of small letters. A small h with a hooked end is probably before 1730. John Bunyan's gothic alphabet and pen writing used double f for a capital, but samplers show the capital we know. Only in the earliest books and samplers will be found the overlapping V's for "double U". The capital A with its cross-stroke at the top was used in early Saxon coins and is common in early samplers.

The slowness of sewing made children form letters backwards more often than they did in writing. With the pen, a fluid feel for the stroke aided memory. Common sampler errors were reversed s, 4, and capital N. b & d, p & q were written and sewn as mirror images of each other. To "mind your p's and q's", also meant, to mind "please & thankyou's".

Alphabet copied from an undated sampler, by A I, c. 1640.

If the alphabet from an early undated sampler by "A I" is compared with the c.1600 horn book or with John Bunyan's primer, the earlier 20/21 letter Latin alphabet is visible. "XYand Z" had for a long time been common in printer's alphabets, but writers' and children's alphabets were unsure whether to include them until the end of the civil war. A change to the use of English in 1653 parish records assumed the common people would read and write in that language.

The supposition that acorn motifs connect with the Stuart monarchy and commemorate Charles II's escape in an oak tree often lead to undated acorn samplers being guessed "mid 17th century". Acorns were popular motifs before and after the 1651 Battle of Worcester. If a confident 24 letter alphabet is found, it is better than acorns to suggest the second half of that century: if a 21 letter alphabet is found or the curious xyz's of contemporary handwriting it is not unreasonable to think it may date from earlier times.

Everything in John Bunyan's "help to Children", including the old gothic capitals, eventually found its way into samplers, but the conjoined letters seldom appear until the end of the eighteenth century.

AI's sampler has acorns, carnations, honeysuckle, daisies, roses and 'Boxers' mixed up with geometric patterns. The striking thing is its SILENCE!

Like many continental samplers, alphabets, dates, name, emblems and ages were demonstrations of embroidery skill composing a tradition for children's samplers. They show, but they do not speak. The inclusion of a moral or pious verse in all its varieties often distinguishes English and thereby American samplers.

The Reformation had turned people away from many old rituals of religion. The holiness of the priesthood, gave place to the authority of Scripture. Protestants were entranced by the English Bible, and enthusiastic to know it well. Teaching children to read and learn Bible verses was a concern that changed samplers profoundly.

English samplers found their voice during the last years of the Commonwealth.

Between the Restoration of Charles II and Queen Anne's death, epigrams and couplets grew into whole verses, copied from scripture and moral literature. Personal invention and choice expressed the sentiments of child and family.

It was a Protestant phenomenon - but more than that. The tradition began among generations that gave their sons Christian names like, "Praise God", "Praise ye all the works of the Lord" and perhaps, "Man is born to trouble as the sparks fly upward." The English were intoxicated with their own language.

The King James version of the Bible merely confirmed translations familiar to Elizabethan England. The Prayer Book in English had also settled into common use. The age-long ignorance of English congregations was shattered by the sound of their own tongue in sacred scripture. Its inspiration astounded the nation. Shakespeare would not have written except that the language of martyred Tyndale and Cranmer rang in his ears.

Verses

The earliest verses were simple moral statements or rhyming couplets, combining learning and religion. Before that time only emblems, alphabets and patterns are known.

A completely new purpose in samplers had already developed. They were no longer catalogues of adult embroidery trials, but tasks for children to begin and finish within a few months; not to be rolled up and kept for reference, but to be displayed as finished memorials to the age of innocence. The name of the child who made the sampler figured prominently. Where this was thought presumptuous, initials were allowed.

Childhood is a timeless place, but the moral lessons of the sampler insisted that the importance of the passing moment should be taken into the child's mind:

This sentiment appeared early:

> *"Dear child delay no time, but with all speed amend;*
> *The longer thou dost live, The nearer to thy end.*   Susannah Ingram's sampler, 1700.

It continued throughout the tradition:

> *"Time is one of the most precious talents in the world, which the author of it has*
> *committed to our management. So precious that he gives it by drops, nor ever affords us two*
> *moments at once, but always takes away one when he lets us have another."*
> Isabella Kay's sampler, 1805.

"he" is the masculine author of the world and of time.

Dates

Adult samplers that recorded favourite motifs to remember and repeat were not dated. There was no purpose dating something that continued each year to form a woman's work-piece of embroidery. But for a single task that marked a particular and important stage in a child's life, it was natural enough to sew a date into the work. Some early samplers declare that the date is that of beginning the work:

> *"Ealli Crygier her work begen IVLY the 8 day 1734. Simon Crygier .*
> *Grateful unto thy parents be, so it gain*
> *Thair second help if thou should'st ned again."*
>
> Simon was probably Ealli's father.

Others as surely tell us when it was finished.

> *"Pray think of me as you pass by,*
> *As you are now, so once was I;*
> *But hear I lye desolved to dust,*
> *In hope to rise among the just.*
> *Isaac Parish. Elizabeth Parish. Jane Parish her work July the fourtinth 1718. Finis."*

Where the date alone is given, the custom was to give the date when the last stitch was put in. In a few cases the dates of both beginning and ending are given. From this and written records it can be known that a sampler took from a few weeks to a year to complete. Occasional and large samplers are known to have taken two years. Four to six months would be the average.

An alteration to pretend an earlier date, easily made by letting three stitches of a six disappear to leave a nought, is probably the work of a later hand interested in making the sampler appear more valuable. A later hand may also add a date to an undated work, but samplers usually have clues that forbid serious deception.

In some samplers it is less obvious that a date was later unpicked by the maker herself. For samplers made after 1700, it is worth looking for a place where the date may once have been sewn. In a few Poor Schools, dates were discouraged, but these were quite unlike samplers from the homes and schools where the traditions began.

As samplers developed into children's apprentice-pieces, age was a badge of merit; part of its purpose to be displayed on a wall of a proud parents' home. When in time the girl grew up, she often inherited it to be hung in her home, recalling her skill, her companions, and her innocence when she was very young. Not uncommonly, the date was an intimacy she no longer wished to give, and her age not something to be bandied about.

Sometimes it can be seen that a sampler had been taken down and the date carefully unpicked, even cut right out, lest a visitor might accurately calculate the lady's present age while he pretended to be admiring the stitches.

The date may be as significant as sewn verses that speak the hopes and fears of the child and the expectations of the age.

In early alphabets, I stood for vowel and consonant, i and j. V was similarly vowel and consonant, u and v. Thus IVLY or IVLI was JULY. The introduction of *j* came into use from the habit of medieval scribes writing money in Latin numbers. Four pence was written jiii d. (denarius) The first lower case *i* had a long tail. Similarly, the initial i in English words was pronounced hard, like justice not soft like interest.

Habit and pronunciation combined to produce *J* and *j*. *I* and *i*.

In the illustration of Hannah and Dorothy Edwards' sampler, the royal monogram appears to be I.R. with the "I" disguised by other stitches and an initial R reversed for symmetry. J had not yet appeared in the sampler alphabet, so "I" in a monogram would signify James II. But the date is 1692, four years after he ran away from England and was deposed in favour of William and Mary. Only a Jacobite family would have sewn James' monogram onto a sampler.

In some cases a sampler text refers directly to a recent historic event. Otherwise, the date and verse taken together may suggest it. A blessing on the sovereign may be coincident with an alarm about the Protestant succession; the Jacobite rebellions of 1715 and 45 for instance, or the unfolding of the French Revolution.

The sampler of Mary Eldrig, made at the time of the first Jacobite rebellion, includes:

> *"God bless the king, preserve the crown,*
> *Defend the church, tread rebells down."*

Samplers of the 1820 and 1830's might show a square-windowed building called the "Queen's Palace" and there was depicted George IV building Buckingham Palace from his mother's home.

The date and the history of its time provide windows from the sampler to the world with which its maker was familiar.

Sarah Baker's sampler declares that it was *"wrought February the 17ᵗʰ day, 17367"*

Protestant Britain continued with the Julian calendar when the rest of Europe changed to the Catholic Gregorian dates. By 1752, when we belatedly conformed, continental dates had diverged considerably from ours, causing all kinds of confusion. We were obliged to lop eleven days from March to adjust. At the same time we ceased to date the beginning of each year on 25ᵗʰ March and adopted the 1st of January.

In the period before that, correspondence was in a muddle; awkward for trade and full of uncertainty. Sarah's sampler simply acknowledges that the date was either 1736 or 1737 according to a changing custom.

The influence of the Puritan spirit on samplers is not easy to disentangle from the Protestant. The Protestant faith embraced a feel for the social equality of decent people, a respect for hard work and learning, and a trust that bible study would declare unquestionably the purposes of God to the world. Tudor and Stuart princesses were well instructed in the literature of European and Classical languages. Royal girls were accomplished scholars; though this liberality barely touched the lives of most women.

The noble habit of placing out daughters to be taught in the homes of other renowned family members, created an ideal adopted by the middle classes of society. Boarding schools, dominated by French influence, prospered in Georgian times.

The Puritan faith, however, suspected that full intellectual education would be a dangerous diversion from the modest piety and domestic virtue that befitted all women. As the Puritan movement broke into ever more sects, the need to keep within the bounds of each peculiar faith persuaded them all to favour obedience over speculation. Believing women were more susceptible to persuasion than men, Puritans avoided boarding schools and preferred giving girls limited teaching within the home, under the command of fathers or husbands. In 1647 Mary Browne married the diarist John Evelyn before she was thirteen.

Milton's unhappy experience of women led him to doubt their understanding of anything but obedience. His poor daughters were taught just enough to be able to read to him in his blindness. They read from French, Italian, or Latin books, passages they were unable to appreciate; and only escaped from this drudgery, by apprenticeship to embroidery. The following sampler verse was commonly called, "Milton's Daughter."

> *"One did commend me to a WIFE both fair and young,*
> *That had French, Spanish and Italian tongue.*
> *I thank'd him kindly and told him I loved none such,*
> *For I thought one tongue for a wife too much.*
> *What! love ye not the learned? Yes, as my life!*
> *A learned Schollar, but not a learned wife."*   Ann Wing's sampler, c1820

The sentiment was too general to be simply thought of as the division between Cavalier and Puritan two hundred years before.

A book of 1631, typical of many, expressed the ideal Puritan woman as *"no busie-bodie … unless it were about her family, needle or sampler."* The conviction that all time was misspent that a girl borrowed from family duties varied according to social class as well as sect. Houses rich enough to have servants, kept their women from coarse work such as cleaning, washing and cooking. This elevated needlework into a polite and pious occupation; never better expressed than in their samplers.

Cromwell's women were keen on embroidery, something natural to his standing as a country gentleman. He opposed Charles in defence of parliamentary authority, and in religious objection to Archbishop Laud's "Popish practices". With his fellows he had a plain man's suspicion of foppery, and trusted the truth of sacred words against superstitious imagery. Such views entitle us to call him Puritan, but in that time the word described extreme sects who were his allies in parliament and the army. He crushed them both, when their extravagant opinions threatened the Commonwealth.

Long & Band Samplers

Puritan attitudes included a love of simplicity. Ostentation in speech, manners and dress were thought to be sinful pride. The education of girls was limited by modesty, and their schooling was often confined to Needlework, reading and prayers. The plainest sects took simplicity so far as to condemn embroidery. Why then did Puritans, who scorned fashionable embroidery, continue to urge their girls to make samplers?

Simply put, it was because making a sampler was no longer necessarily a prelude to embroidery. For some it was a farewell to childhood, a gift to a parent or friend, an intimation of mortality, or a study of reading and the quiet road to salvation particularly set out for women. Strict Puritan sects honoured diligence as much as modesty.

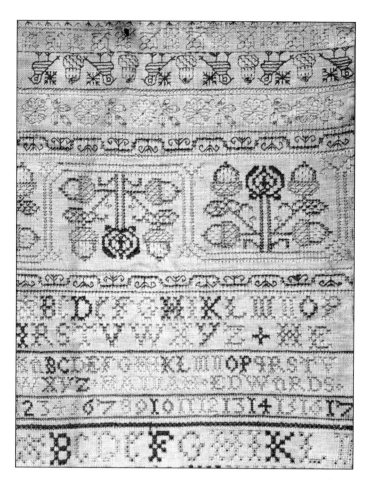

The top of a Long Sampler; Hannah & Dorothy Edwards, 1692.
Bands, Alphabets, Numbers, Acorn and bird motifs. Worked from both ends.

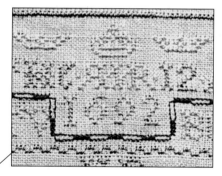

The Royal Monogram R I.

The bottom of the same sampler.
N.B. White work and the "IR" royal monogram.

Typical Bands in a Long Sampler, Elizabeth Clayton, 1668.
Birds, deer, frogs, rabbits ?, acorn, carnation, strawberry, grape ?; and "boxers" with their posies.

In the white work of cuffs and collars for plain gowns, or in under-linen, Puritan families found a field for the demonstration of fidelity, patience, fine work and skill. Patterns, damasks, pulled thread and lace-work, stiff-ironed bodices and the clean decency of linen, gave grace to the dress of men and women and showed meticulous care more than gaudy ornamentation.

White-work pieces were included in many samplers during that century.

A 17th C. White-work linen sampler, with drawn & cutwork, satin, backstitch and needlepoint lace.
Courtesy of St Fagans National History Museum. The right/centre figure is a mermaid with comb and looking glass; the left most probably Judith and her maid with the head of Holofernes. Another English white-work sampler of a similar date in the Fitzwilliam Museum, Cambridge certainly has these two emblems.

Judith was a beautiful and strictly pious widow. When Nebuchadnezzar sent troops to punish Judah, Judith beguiled the Assyrian general Holophernes, cut off his head, and smuggled it into Bethulia hidden in a food basket. She saved the city. The moral is that beauty and charm can bewilder men; but women must be bound by strict laws of honour and of God. As the tale of Delilah is a warning to men; the story of Judith is an example for courageous women, to value beauty and submit to piety. Mermaids also entice men to their doom. The world knows men can be weak and foolish.

Women, used to many humiliations, might find consolation in either emblem.

White thread did not bring out the alphabets, numbers and texts that young girls sewed; so in honour of learning, pastel colours were allowed in Puritan samplers. Even a few emblems taken from nature might be allowed, since the allegory of nature showed the will of God, only a shade less precisely than sacred scripture.

"I read his awful name emblazon'd high
With golden letters in th'illumin'd sky.
Nor less, the mystic characters I see
Wrought in each flower; inscribed on ev'ry tree.
In ev'ry leaf that trembles on the breeze
I hear the voice of God among the trees."
Lydia Ann Temple's sampler, 1821.

In England and America, Quaker schools produced some of the most striking and patient samplers, just as the Shakers and the Amish produced furniture and quilts whose elegant simplicity and usefulness admonishes more showy artists.

The sampler story is entering here the world of the honest artisan and the skilled labourer as well as the world of aristocrats and the rich commercial-classes. Samplers and learning itself were rare exceptions in the world of the poor

17th century adult samplers, had their emblems sewn from any edge of the canvas for they lived as separate examples, not as part of one continuous piece. They are sometimes called Spot or Random samplers. But the children's work developing in that century was quite different. As soon as the Sampler became a set task for young girls, with a beginning and an end, the elements in it were composed within bands, each one a lesson and example. It then combined common stitches that were thought useful for embroidery; and enabled a child, already past first instruction with the needle, to complete her sampler in a year.

Names

The child's name was sewn either at the beginning or toward the end, when the completion of the sampler was predictable. A date was inserted, usually marking the day of the final stitch. Now and again a teacher's name would be included. Otherwise it was common to name the parents; as an honour or in hope for their approval of the gift. Less commonly the place of habitation was given, or the name of the school in which it was done, if not in the sewing circle of the family.

Inscribed texts were usually short and were repeated throughout the country. A common example from 1702 was:

"Abigail Muns is my name and England is my nation and
Aldersgate Street is my dwelling place and Christ is my salvation."

An admonition often sewn was, *"Remember now thy Creator in the days of thy Youth"*, and sometimes the stern warning that followed it; *"while the evil Days come not, nor the Years draw nigh when thou shalt say, I have no pleasure in them"*.

A more child-like verse was *".................. is my name and with my needle I wrote the same, And if I had been better, I would have mended every letter."*

The Lord's Prayer was often copied.

Of the Ten Commandments, one commonly stands on its own: "Honour thy Father and thy Mother that thy days may be long in the Land which the Lord thy God giveth thee."

Parents were very often honoured in children's samplers.

Governess and Instructress

Among similar samplers from the time, Mary Wright's in 1669 had the verse:

"Mary Wright is my name
And with my needl I wrought the same
And Goody Readd was my dame."

Goodwoman or "Goody" was a title used for widows; a skilled family friend perhaps or one who maybe ran a Dame School where Mary learned Religion, Polite Conversation, Reading and Needlework. In later times most Dame Schools degenerated into child-minders for working women. Their girls would not have been taught to make samplers.

Girls from affluent families were often taught at home by the girl's mother or under a governess or sewing instructress. Sometimes this is clearly acknowledged in the work, but it may need to be interpreted.

A huge sampler sewn in 1799 is crammed with figures and verses, and signed, *"Elizabeth Jackson, aged 10, taught by her mother."*

In 1759 Hester Woodward added, "*Anne Brewster Governes*" to her sampler.

A Scots sampler of 1745 by Betty Pleanderleath, just adds, "*Mrs. Setons*", to acknowledge her instructress.

Elizth Wildsmith (1748), Sarah Beamodeine (1753), Elizabeth Oxley (1754), Ann Lock (1761), and Mary Portus (1764) all declare they were "*Taught by Mary Hewart*". Probably "Mrs Huit" (spelling accepted) who taught Janet Anderson in 1815 was of the same family. Such acknowledgements are interesting additions to samplers of the time.

In 1844, a pretty sampler with trees and a house contained the verse:
"*Esther Cranstone is my name, With my needle I work the same,*
And by my needle you may see   What pains my governess took by me."

About this time Charlotte Bronte was learning the duties and indignities of the position.

A very busy sampler labels a shepherd and shepherdess among its figures. Alongside a twined serpent on the appropriate tree:
"*Adam and Eve, Whilst innocent in Paradise were Plast,*
But soon the Serpent, by his wiles, the happy pair disgraced."
Beneath is a bigger tree and under it, two other figures with the legend:
"*No burial did these Babes of any Man Receev*
Til Robinredbreast, painfully, did cover them with leaves."

The signature is "*Mary Lloyd in the 13 Year of her Age 1827 by J, Woodhouse*" and an auctioneer described the sampler as "Mary Lloyd and J. Woodhouse," as if worked by two girls. This is quite unlikely, and the initial, in place of a full Christian name, strongly suggests that Mary Lloyd was taught by J. Woodhouse. Perhaps J. Woodhouse was a young woman, not herself well taught in much but Needlework. Errors of spelling and syntax would not stand in the way of either pupil or teacher, while they were handsome and had confident and agreeable natures.

Edwina Ehrman, Curator of Dress & Decorative Art at the Museum of London, and Kathy Staples, of The Curious Works Press have identified ten samplers from about the year 1700, sewn under the instruction of a widow, Judeth Hayle. Four more, probably taught under her daughter after Judeth's death, repeat the meticulous detail that is wholly convincing of a single discipline.

It must be uncertain how any girl learned the needlework that enabled her to make a sampler. Seldom was the skill developed solely within one sewing circle, either of the family or of the school. It brings the child to mind, when something within the sampler points to what is most likely among all the possibilities.

Alphabets and Numbers were written in bands across the width; the text perhaps in bands further down the sampler. Such was the horror of wasting cloth that words were sometimes crushed up or broken at the end of each band. Numbers from 1 to 0 were sewn, and continued for as long as it was necessary not to waste the space left in the band.

Different patterns and skills were contained in similar horizontal bands of floral garlands, geometric patterns and repeated emblems; acorns or hands, frogs or little birds. Acorns might mean great oaks from little acorns grow, a suitable admonition for children to take pains with their work

In Catholic Europe the winepress symbol was an allegory of Christ's Passion. They also used the device of a giant bunch of grapes hung from a pole on the shoulders of two men. Called "The Spies of Canaan", the symbol portrayed the men who had gone into the Promised Land and brought back to Moses evidence of its great fertility. By shaping the bunch not unlike a great heart it became a code for the Mass. In England it took another century before the emblems of Christ's Passion replaced the importance of the Old Testament in samplers. The Spies of Canaan straddle the two testaments and appear in English samplers, but not until the end of the eighteenth century.

The Spies of Canaan symbol from Elizabeth Woodward's sampler, aged 12, 1790.

A feature of English long samplers were curious little manikins, called "Boxers" because they stood with arms and legs like boxers facing each other in a fight. Curlicues sprouted from their joints. One hand held a feather-like object as if offering a gift. Perhaps the emblem arose from one figure giving the palm to the other, but its import is unsure. In the same way emblems of Adam and Eve misconstrued classic pictures of the Judgement of Paris and imagine the forbidden fruit to have been an apple. The Biblical story of Adam and Eve was the commonest and well understood device on English samplers.

Spinning and weaving were female domestic arts, and samplers were sewn on cloth from household looms 7 to 9 inches wide. The length varied according to the number of bands wanted to complete the piece. Children's samplers were therefore much longer than wide. Its shape had been determined by its early purpose to be kept rolled up in the work box. Either side of 1700 a change overtook children's samplers; the change from Long Band Samplers to Picture and Inscription Samplers.

Picture and Inscription Samplers

A noticeable change in the shape of samplers occurred after weavers from the Netherlands and France were driven, exiled, into England. Persecution of Protestants followed the revocation of the Edict of Nantes (1685) and the successes of the Catholic Counter-reformation. Wider cloths, with even threads and tensions became readily available. Industrialisation of an English cottage industry had begun. The narrow or long-sampler fell out of fashion and was replaced by a shape with the dimensions of a picture. The composition of bands ended, and the outline of the sampler was first marked with a border made by a patterned or undulating garland. The leafed stem of the garland held flowers or fruits within the bays; and joining it up to meet symmetrically at the corners, was beyond the unaided skill of a child.

The work was done in counted stitches, and even by a single error the plan would be overthrown. One of the common bands of the old kind of sampler had been just such a garland, but in transferring to its purpose as a framework for the new shape, it stretched out into waves rather than rectangular bays. In Scotland where the Band Sampler, even in its new shape, continued to the end, the old garland tradition continued with it. But England abandoned the Band Sampler with the Long Sampler, accepting the new form, with an enthusiasm that left few exceptions after 1730.

Everything within the border garland had to be planned; a space left for the alphabet and the verse, which now tended to be longer; a space for birds, trees, figures or other emblems made in symmetrical pairs for balance; a space for the dedication or the child's name, age and the year of completion. Such a work may be called an Inscription Sampler; and was, until the end of samplers, the commonest style.

From the earliest times children well instructed and clever sought to choose emblems that might be combined to resemble a Picture. But a proper Picture Sampler had as its centre an embroidered idyllic scene marked in pencil or pricked out in soot by a talented adult. It was as close as children could get to the embroideries their mother's generation made in the sewing circle. It demanded artistic initiative only in the asymmetrical natural scene, and the girl chose the stitches that would give the drawing colour and life. Care and obedience enabled counted stitch to discipline the rest of the child's sampler. For two or three generations a Picture Sampler was the ideal form, and they are today the most desirable.

The inclusion of an Adam & Eve motif, or a House, within an Inscription Sampler may make it closely resemble a Picture Sampler, but the distinction can be made. In searching for an easier goal, and in descent to lower social orders, Sampler Stitch slowly supplanted the long and short, the stem, and satin stitches, the French knots and Algerian eyes that were part of early Picture Samplers.

By the end of the century, sampler-making had in many cases descended to the sole use of this one stitch - Cross Stitch. It had begun as a Marking Stitch to label the household linen, and was of little use for anything else. A cross stitch sampler was not a prelude to embroidery. Mostly it was a task in which young ladies learned patience, perseverance, a fine hand and handsome posture. These accomplishments inspired proper admiration, from family, friends and young gentlemen.

A typical Inscription Sampler. Adam & Eve plus symmetrical emblems, etc. Thomasine Denton, aged 8, 1824.

A typical Picture Sampler. Elizabeth Lammiman, 1832. The influence of a fashion for Berlin Wool-work is already apparent in the picture.

The Origins of Sampler Verses

Pictures or motifs left room within the garland border for the dedication, the alphabets, numbers, and verses. The verses began to expand, and longer poems came to be included. They were chosen from a greater variety of sources. Before 1670 samplers without verses far outnumber those with them. By 1690 verses or a moral sentence appear in half of them.

By 1700, samplers without verses are the exception. Most verses come from the Bible or Church traditions; rather fewer originate in homely or proverbial couplets, and the same amount from School and copybook traditions. A smaller group reflect other literature, and sayings more ethical than religious.

By 1736 familiar hymns begin to appear in the verses of English samplers. The Scottish Psalter of 1635 had metricated the psalms, and profoundly encouraged congregational chanting and singing. English hymns and English samplers show the influence. Martha Sharpe in 1711 sewed a couplet from that Psalter:

"Psalm the 23
The Lord is only my support, and he that doth me feed;
How can I then lack anything, whereof I stand in need."

Mary Magick's sampler in 1721 gives part of Psalm 40 from the same Psalter.
"I waited long, I sought the Lord,
And patiently did beare
To me at length, he did accord
My voice and cry to hear.
He pluck me from the lake so deep,
Out of the mire and clay,
And on a rock he set my feet,
And he did guide my way.
To me he taught a psalm of praise.

The usefulness of this style with children, led samplers to simplify and compose Bible verses into rhyming couplets to aid retention in the memory:
"Lord give me wisdom to direct my ways, I ask not riches nor yet length of days."
Solomon's Prayer.
"Love (Fear) the Lord and he will be A tender father unto thee."

"See how the lilies flourish wite and fair, See how the ravens fed from Heaven are.
Then ne'er distrust your god for cloth or bread, Whilst lilies flourish and the
ravens fed."

It was now more common to feature the whole of the Ten Commandments, and they too were sometimes metricated in rhyming couplets.

"Have thou no other Gods but me,
Unto no Image bow thou the knee;
Take not the name of God in vain,

Do not the Sabbath day profane;
Honour thy father and thy mother (too),
And see that thou no murder do*;
from whoredom keep thee chaste (and clean),
And steal not tho thy steat be m(ean);
Of false report bear not the blot,
What is thy neighbours covet not.
Cristtain Gilchrist is her(e) seen."

Scots sampler of Cristtain Gilchrist, 1745.

* Children's reading usually distinguished "murder" from "kill" in the sixth commandment.

The English Bible if not the Authorised Version still dominated sampler verses.

Within this awful volume lies The mystery of mysteries.
Happiest they of human race, To whom their God hath given grace
To read to fear, to hope, to pray, To lift the latch, to force the way;
And better had they ne'er been born Than read to doubt, or read to scorn."

Frances Roe's sampler. 1848

Among many verses copied exactly was this prayer of Agur, from the book of Proverbs:
"Two things have I required of thee; deny them me not before I die:
Remove far from me vanity and lies; lest I be full and deny thee and say, Who is the Lord?
Or lest I be poor, and steal, and take the name of my God in vain."

The story of Zacheus climbing a tree to see Jesus go by was popular in samplers as a parable for children to realise the persistence needed to worship Christ.

John Bunyan metricated the ten commandments in his "Country Rhimes for Children", and lines very close to it appeared in samplers. His Puritan faith raised antagonism and his parables in verse, "Divine Emblems", were too adult in tone to enter children's memory and be copied accurately. A book of fables by John Gay, 1727, was in this more successful. In 1720 Dr Isaac Watts published a book called, "Divine Songs for Children". These simple and memorable moral tales gained widespread popularity, and a wealth of sampler verses were copied exactly from them over the following hundred years.

Isaac Watts' summary of the Commandments is:

"With all thy soul love god above, And as thyself thy neighbour love."

Ann Clowser's sampler 1723

And from Christ's Golden Rule is:

"Be you to others kind and tru, As you'd have others be to you"

Mary Brewitt's sampler 1725

Watt's poem, "How doth the little busy bee, improve each shining hour" finished with:
"In works of labor or of skill I would be busy too;
For Satan finds some mischief still For idle hands to do."

"In books, or work or healthful play, Let my first years be past,
That I may give for ev'ry day Some good account at last." Mary Mustoo, 1726

The 18th century respect for Duty and acceptance of consequence shifted visibly in samplers as Gentle Jesus became more axxepted than the wrath of an Old Testament God. It is exemplified by the most popular of all sampler verses, said to be composed by the Reverend John Newton for his niece, Elizabeth Catlett.

"Jesus permit thy gracious name to stand, As the first effort of an infant hand,
And while her fingers on the canvas move Incline her tender heart to seek thy love.
With thy dear children let her have a part, And write thy name, thyself, upon her heart."

The first example of this was sewn in 1782 by Lucy Smith. Before that time and after it, a sterner message was prominent; that life was full of traps, and that the guiding reason of adult admonition was necessary to escape damnation. Reason and teaching was emphasised more than faith and hope. The Romantic Movement in literature which blossomed with Wordsworth was yet to influence sampler verse.

The Age of Reason preferred children to listen to Alexander Pope, whose Moral Essays included this from Epistle 1.

" Tis education forms the tender mind. Just as the twig's bent, the tree's inclin'd."   Hannah Janney, 1785.

In 1791 Mary Goffe wrote, unpunctuated, the whole of Pope's "Universal Prayer" in her Charity School sampler. Much of it is beyond a child's understanding, composed of tortured Catholicism and the hope that new scientific disciplines would make God's purposes clear in a better understanding of Nature. Verses 8 and 10, standing articulate on their own in samplers, are more commonly quoted from a very quotable poet.

"If I am right, thy grace impart still in the right to stay;
If I am wrong Oh! Teach my heart to find that better way."

Teach me to feel another's woe, to hide the fault I see;
That mercy I to others shew, that mercy shew to me."

Pope's "Essay on Man" is also quoted:
"Vice is a monster of so frightful mien
As to be hated needs but to be seen;
Yet seen too oft, familiar with her face,
We first endure, then pity, then embrace."

Jane Pipe's sampler, 1832

"The lamb thy riot dooms to bleed today,
Had he thy reason would he skip and play;
Pleas'd to the last, he crops the flow'ry food,
And licks the hand just rais'd to shed his blood.   Sarah Frishmuth's sampler, 1743

Disobedient children were admonished to, "kiss the rod".

Pope particularly addressed himself to women readers. They had been largely ignored by the learned poets who preceded him. His critics sneered at him for it, and later ages accused him of patronising women because he retained tender, masculine prejudices. His women readers of the time were grateful to be noticed at all, and welcomed his talent.

The rules of God, nature and society, were placed before hopes of redemption. By 1800 more sampler verses were attributing salvation to Christ's infinite mercies.

Apart from the Bible, Isaac Watt's songs formed the most persistent source of sampler verse. They explored many themes about childhood, home, duty and religion; and they did it in tender and also in unblinking style.

> *"Have we not heard what dreadful plagues Are threatened by the Lord*
> *To them that break their father's laws, And mock their mother's word.*
> *What heavy guilt upon them lies, How cursed is their name:*
> *The ravens shall pick out their eyes, Eagles shall eat the same."* Bithiah Townsend,1740

Significantly differing verses arose from the copy lines set by Writing Masters. Copybook lines, learned by all who were taught to write, were repeated meticulously in samplers, familiar as folk wisdom. Aphorisms, traditional to Writing Masters from before the Tudors, were copied in every corner of the kingdom and, when they appear in girls' samplers, suggest the work was done at school. Most originated in "The Sayings of the Wise Cato", and breathed an unreligious air, less Christian than Stoic. Their flavour of second century Rome is identifiable again and again in sampler verse.

"If breath were made for every man to buy,   *The poor could not live and the rich would not die."*

"Children like tender osiers take the bow   *And as they first are fashioned always grow."*

"Learn to contemn all praise betimes,   *For flatt'ry is the nurse of crimes."*

Virtue's our safeguard and our guiding star   *That stirs up reason when our senses err."*

"Constraint in all things makes the pleasure less,   *Sweet is the love that comes with willingness."*

"Money, like manure, does no good until it is spread."

"Despair of nothing that you would attain,   *Unwearied diligence your point will gain."*
"Experience is gained without much cost,   *Read men and books, then practise what thou knowest."*

"In prosperity friends will be plenty,   *But in adversity not one in twenty."*

But Samplers were, above all, a folk-art; and memorable or stark or feminine or pious, verses were loved and copied from one teacher to another. Some were composed with a personal sense of humour.

> *"When beauty is adorn'd with grace,*
> *There's a jewell in a Christall case."*   Grace Fowle's sampler 1711.

In 1748 one of Martha Brooks' family composed a verse for her sampler that talked of streams and rivers; and others have made moral verses that the name suggested. Rebekah Flower's verse in 1785 begins, "*Give unto God the flower of thy youth.*"

Seven year old Anne Hathaway in 1797 recognised the coincidence of her name with that of Shakespeare's wife by quoting a line from his Titus Andronicus; "*Fair Philomel, she but lost her tongue, and in a tedious sampler sewed her mind.*" (Titus' daughter had her hands cut off as well, and so seemed quite unable to accuse the man who raped her.)

Susannah Garden's verse in 1836 is, of course, about the beauty of flowers.

Now and again, a wry sally shows a confident and adventurous heart.

> *"Adam alone in paradise did grieve,*
> *And thought Eden a desert without Eve;*
> *Until God, pitying his lonesome state,*
> *Crowned all his riches with a lovely mate.*
> *What reason then has man to slight or flout her;*
> *That could not live in paradise without her.*" Mary Batty's sampler, aged 9, 1777

Rebuses and riddles were used, though rarely:

> *"My first to music gives expression,*
> *Yet often is produced by fright;*
> *My second I must make confession,*
> *Will send you to the shades of night.*
> *My first and second rightly placed,*
> *Behold at once this nation's pride,*
> *Whose memory has long since been grac'd*
> *By honours that have never died"*

When Caroline Mary Peacher sewed this in 1804, a *Shake* was a trill in the singing voice, to give emotional emphasis. Somewhere, her riddle still gives the pleasure she hoped for when she sewed it.

In 1826, Ann Welch sewed "*Keep the commandments and Live.*" The couplet that followed was made into a puzzle simply by leaving out all punctuation and vowels:

PRSVRYPRFCTMN&VRKPTHSPRCPTSTN

(Praise every perfect man & ever keep these precepts ten)

Here, from 1749, is one of at least three acrostic samplers. All the things mentioned in the verses appear as emblems about it.

> *A virgin that's industrious merits praise:*
> *N ature she imitates in various ways;*
> *N ow forms the pink, now gives the rose its blaze.*

Young buds she folds in tender leaves of green,
O mits no shade to beautify the scene.
U pon the canvas, see the letters rise,
N eatly they shine with intermingled dies,
G lide into words, and strike us with surprise.

Sampler verse could be light hearted or resigned, though most often it was a solemn and an admonishing finger that was wagged at the girls.

Elizabeth De'ath in 1771 sewed this sombre but appropriate verse which was probably composed in her family.

"Behold thy end ere thou begin;
Have mind on Death and fear to sin.
For death will reap where Life hath sown
And Life will spring where Death hath mown."

Punctuation and Spelling

Not all errors in the stitching of words were the child's fault. What they copied was often from memory or other samplers, and not from books.

Punctuation was different from what it is today, and few instructors of needlework had the conventions to hand. All substantive nouns once had capitals, so god did not, and it was arguable whether Heaven should. The rules took time to establish.

In 1766 Dinah Deaves sewed consistent punctuation in her sampler verse. Earlier, few girls would have understood it, and afterwards it was no commoner than it would be today. Before the same date, idiosyncratic spelling should not be taken for ignorance. English was once spelt as the author pleased, and the same word might be spelt three ways on the same Bible page without any difficulty or doubt in its reading. The authorised version bred a notion that such a thing as *Correct* spelling existed. Teachers slowly began to eliminate phonetic spellings that mirrored regional pronunciation. Smiths wrote their names thus, while Smythes, being more affluent, had documents to prove forefathers had written their names so, two hundred years before. The advent of Dr Johnson's Dictionary in 1755 eliminated many, but not all, common variations in spelling.

For a time honor/honour, labor/labour, did not distinguish fashions on one or the other side of the Atlantic. From the printing of Webster's American Dictionary in 1806 particular American conventions such as center/color began to be established.

The traditional shape of an English sampler from a gentle or comfortable family had settled down, and the Band Sampler had been discarded. The new shape framed an Inscription or a Picture Sampler according to social confidence and family choice. Wealth perhaps, but elegance certainly, persuaded some families to favour Picture Samplers. Infant simplicity and young fingers favoured Inscription Samplers, but maybe suspicion of extravagance, and a dour, obedient piety inspired the same choice

Somewhere in all these elements, a vision of the little girl who made any particular sampler may be dimly visible. Whatever the sampler, the poignancy expressed cannot be read except by considering the age of the child; the purpose of the work; and the emotional change that was signalled by this rite of passage that took a child onto the threshold of womanhood.

Before describing the limitations imposed on many poor Victorian girls, it should be understood why, where, and in what conditions, girls of all sort made samplers.

An unfinished Picture Sampler, Mary Ann Kerbys, 1809, showing the drawing that was to be filled.
Death, more likely than irresolution, left the work unfinished, and if so, the verse was prophetic.

Lydia Clark, aged 11, 1838.
A common plea from private schools, that the gift of learning was received from the parents' care

Bible and Alphabet. Catherine Pettit 1798.

**An elaborate sampler for a seven year old girl.
Sarah Sisson 1805.**

A typical American sampler. R. Wilson c 1800.
Above the sheaves of wheat are two "Ackworth" emblems.
Courtesy of Scaramanga Antiques.

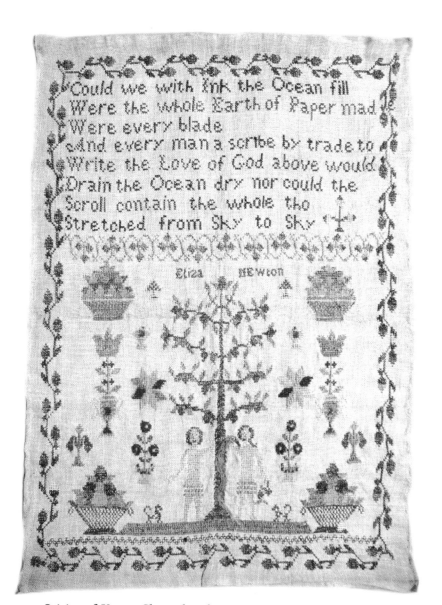

Origins of Verse. Cheap thread on poor canvas, Eliza Newton sewed c1810 a standard sampler with a misremembered verse. She was neither rich nor poor.

The words and sentiments inspired Walter de la Mare to write his poem, "The Scribe." In 1917 Frederick Lehman found something similar scribbled on the wall of a Californian insane asylum, and made from it a popular hymn, "The Love of God". Similar words and sentiments are ascribed to Rabbi Mayer, a cantor of Worms in Germany, 1096.

It would have been known in many times and languages. Folk literature has no copyright, and changes as it passes down the generations. Eliza's model was perhaps:

Could we with Ink the Oceans fill,   Were the whole Earth of Paper made,
A Quill each Reed, each Twig a Blade,   And every Man a Scribe by Trade,
To write the Love of God above   Would drain the Oceans dry,
Nor could the Scroll contain the whole   Tho' stretched from Sky to Sky.

In 1938, grubby boys thought it very witty to chant a parody: "If all the world was paper, and all the seas were ink,
                                            If all the trees were bread and cheese, what would we have to drink?"

Chapter 6
A FAREWELL TO INNOCENCE

"The rose is red, the grass is green, The days are past that I have seen.
My friends, when you these lines do see, In reading them, remember me.
And when the bell begins to toll, The Lord have mercy on my soul,"

Ruth Little's sampler, aged 9, 1766

THE AGE OF THE CHILD

The child's age began to appear on samplers soon after the new traditions began. Age was as significant on samplers as it would be on an epitaph. Now and again the Latin, "Aetat" or its abbreviation AE stands for "Aged" on both.

A sampler showing an age of eight or less is unlikely to have been made at school. A class at school would hope to have six or more children all ready and able at the same time. Before the ages of ten to thirteen, that would not be forthcoming when instructing the making of a sampler; and the purpose of it had traditions that most teachers would be reluctant to think appropriate for children who could not yet recite their alphabet.

But a single child, under her mother's instruction would begin to sew alongside her as soon as she was able; and if calm, and persistent might by the age of seven develop all the skills required to copy the stitches of a sampler. Some children are remarkably dextrous. The bright eyes and nimble fingers of eight year old children made them employable in the tiny, delicate piercing of the cock on pocket watches, and the assembly of miniature chains that drove the verge movements.

A mother, proud of her daughter's precocious skills, could encourage the making of a sampler earlier than usual. Five years of age is about the lower limit, but samplers by seven or eight year olds are not uncommon. Pride tempted parents to anticipate the sampler's proper time. The same impatience leads children today to anticipate their teens.

In many families living between richness and poverty, a young girl would have worked long hours with her needle before she made her principal sampler. Most of her needlework was the hemming and edging and buttonholing and sewing that made and mended the household linen.

The principal sampler was not usually her first essay into colour, but something to look forward to and treasure as a token of growing confidence. It was a coming of age; something unrepeatable. Life on the other side of it was looked to with tremulous hope, and to repeat it would imply that passing through the first time had been something of a disappointment.

As education for girls advanced, the inscription or picture sampler came, well past a girl's ABC, when she was able to read and understand longer verses than those common in the seventeenth century. ABC was nevertheless the traditional way to begin; and though a few girls would have made preliminary Alphabet or Text samplers while very young, it was usual to make a grander sampler as a certificate that she was approaching an important stage in her growing up.

That is why so many were made in the years that herald puberty, the eleventh or twelfth years of a girl's life. At the age of thirteen, Juliet met Romeo for the first time. Most picture samplers were made when the approach to womanhood and married love was thrillingly close. Destiny, duty, overwhelming enlightenment, the prospect of love and the inevitable dangers of motherhood, whirled around the girls' minds; so much closer to sense and sensibility than any proper boy could have been at the same age.

A dramatic change makes girls suddenly aware of their bodies and of fateful adult purposes. Boys continue boyish manners and pursuits for many years yet, but for girls innocence is over and commitment awaits. Girls are immediately older, more sensible perhaps, and more vulnerable.

On her twelfth birthday a girl reached the customary and legal age of consent. The poor were open to a predatory commerce in prostitution, and the rich to the dynastic exploitation of marriage alliances. That condition remained throughout the period during which needlework samplers were made, and was not effectively altered until the Criminal Law Amendment Act of 1885. Most samplers were sewn during the years either side of twelve, and by girls who were well aware that their social position hinged on this fixed distinction. The sampler verses they wrought were chosen to accommodate a wider and wilder emotional content.

The prospect of death was also close to a girl twelve years old. She would be fortunate if both her parents still lived, and she was likely to have seen the burial of more than one of her siblings. Childbirth took off baby and mother alarmingly often. Combining a farewell to youth with the sober contemplation of death was a natural stage in a girl's awareness. Many samplers warned girls not to presume upon the passing delights of youth and beauty:

> *"Gay dainty flowers go swiftly to decay,*
> *Poor wretched life's small portion flies away.*
> *We eat, we sleep, but lo, Anon,*
> *Old age steals on us never thought upon."*
>
> Mary Wakeling's sampler, 1742.

It is not surprising to find death a subject of sampler verse, for it is the persistent strain of poetry, even when the apparent subject is "Daffodils." The sampler's obsession with death began quite early. Many sampler devices originated in Emblem Books popular in the reign of Elizabeth. In 1718 Elizabeth Matron's sampler copied parts of a verse in the Emblem Book of Francis Quarles (1592 - 1644)

> *Like to the damask rose you see, Or like the blossom on the tree,*
> *Or like the dainty flower of May, Or like the morning of the day,*
> *Or like the sun, or like the shade, Or like the gourd that Jonas had,*
> *Even so is Man, whose thread is spun, Drawn out and cut and so is done.*
> *The rose withers, the blossom blasteth; The flower fades, the morning hasteth;*
> *The sun he sets, the shadow flies, The gourd consumes, and Man he dies.*

In samplers, this resignation was usually softened by consolation uniting the shortness of life, the length of eternity, and the necessity of salvation.

"There is a calm for those who weep,
A rest for weary Pilgrims found;
They softly lie, and sweetly sleep
Low in the ground."   Name unknown, 1755

The following verse is starkly humanist; as rational as the poems of Alexander Pope (1688-1744), who was second only to Isaac Watts (1674-1748) in popularity with sampler makers.

"Death at a distance we but slightly fear,
He brings his terrors a he draws more near.
Through poverty, pain, slav'ry, we drudge on,
The worst of beings better please than none.
No price too dear to purchase life and breath;
The heaviest burdens easier borne than death." Kitty Rayner's sampler, 1793

But many sampler verses went beyond this in employing chilling terrors of corruption to frighten young girls from the paths of sin. That shocks us. It is not clear at what age children should face adult realities, but times past thought it came at an age when now we begin to teach them the techniques of sexual intercourse. They thought seven years of age was not too early to acquaint them with damnation. Between Then and Now there was a more sensitive age, reluctant to end innocence; that spoke gently of things that thoughts but tenderly touch. Here are the terrors sewn long ago:

"This sampler my name shall ever have
When I am dead and in my grave.
The greedy worms my body eat,
Then you shall read my name complate."   Jane Mabank's sampler, 1737

And must this body die? this mortal frame decay,
And must these active limbs of mine lie mould'ring in the clay,
And there for to remain until Christ doth please to come."
                                        Barbara Baner's sampler   1812

Less flesh-creeping, yet still stern and sobering is the following example.

"In the sad morn of blooming youth
The various threads I drew,
And pleas'd beheld the finished piece
Rise glowing to my view.
Thus when bright youth shall charm no more
And age shall chill my blood,
May I review my life and say,
*Behold! my works were good."*Margaret Liddle's sampler c.1800

Why do we recoil from sampler verses that are heavily pious or morbid, when both are true reflections of their age? Yet we do. To make a collection of samplers complete, it should reflect the truths of necessity as well as the consolations girls learned while busy with their needles. If prettiness, fine skill, or fastidiousness quite obscures the living fingers that made the sampler, they tell only part of the story of its making. Are we, who look upon their work, less resolute than they?

Our own obsessions arise from the belief that unwanted pregnancies stem from ignorance; theirs from dread of more appalling risks waiting for the eternal souls of young girls. The remedy in either case has been to force-feed children with knowledge beyond their powers to digest. It is not kind to strangle innocence with the knotted anxieties of old men; but the intention was as benevolent as ours.

Acceptance and resolution are expressed by Faith Walker's sampler of 1803.

"Teach me to live that I may dread The grave as little as my bed,"

If teaching could bring calm enlightenment to the bounding innocence of childhood, before age, aches and weariness brought resignation, the tone of that verse would appear more acceptable. The lesson girls had to accept was sometimes expressed with terrors that pinned their imagination like a biology specimen. Between that and illusion, reality had to be faced.

In many churchyards, only the graves of the rich had headstones. The poor had no markers at all. While walking each Sunday between the wooden markers of the prosperous dead, children saw epitaphs already illegibly decayed. While engaged in the long conventional task of making a sampler, the girls were very aware they were sewing a memorial; that learning to mark linen, they were also marking Time. Needle and thread made their own tiny marks on the canvas of eternity.

"When this you see remember mee, Elizabeth Wiber, aged 9 years. 1748
"This was made for them to see, That liveth after me, Barbara Hunsicker, 1831"

Little needle-women would wonder on whose wall their sampler might hang, and hope that in the home of parents or friends it would perpetuate their hopes and faith. More and more, these thoughts would merge with the idea that their sampler should be a gift in gratitude, to parents if they still lived, or to friends. Many arose from the fond separations of school life, and the companions who shared it.

Some samplers were sewn at home, safe in the sewing circle of family and friends. Many girls also learned their letters there, taught by relatives or governesses. Away at boarding school, homesickness sent other girls to bed crying in the dormitories, and made friendships more intense. Even where the name of a school is not sewn into the sampler the patterns and verses of school samplers may make it apparent that they were not made in the home.

If samplers of two sisters are alike it merely means that they shared the same teacher, family or school. Hannah Turner in 1719 sewed a central lozenge with its verse and other verses going from one side to the other of the diamond. Jane Parish in 1718 had sewed the same, unusual pattern, the same royal monogram, the same stitching, and the same poem. It was one believed to be by Queen Elizabeth herself when arguing what stand to take in the religious controversy on transubstantiation.

"Christ was the word that spake it,
He took the bread and break it,
And what that word did make it,
That I believe and take it".

Though only two samplers with this structure seem to have survived, and the school is unknown, such similarities show they were instructed by one instructor who had an individual model for her girls. It is sensible to infer that a work was done at school rather than home if it contains verses that were popular because they were part of the discipline of schools.

At Christmas, pupils took home a sample of their Writing lessons. Often it included a copied letter from the principal to the parents, assuring them their child was properly grateful for the chance to be educated, and trusting parents would be pleased by the efforts of the child and the success of the teaching. Hope was expressed that this evidence would ensure the principal had the pleasure of greeting their child at the start of the following year.

As early as 1709 the teachers of school needlework began to introduce a similar advertisement into their pupils' samplers.

> *"Next unto God, dear parents I address*
> *Myself to you in humble thankfulness,*
> *For all your care and charge on me bestowed,*
> *The means of learning unto me allowed.*
> *Go on, I pray, and let me still pursue*
> *Those golden arts the vulgar never knew."*
>
> Susan Slater's sampler

When the sampler comes from a comfortable family, their women would have had some schooling; and simple literacy was taken for granted. But the greater mass of the population was too poor to know literacy or embroidery. Even as their ambitions grew, they were mostly without the benefit of free schools to help them aspire to the style of life that was expressed well in the samplers of more fortunate families.

In the first half of the nineteenth century, Sarah Eales was a poor girl at school. Her sampler shows the usual capital alphabet and numbers and a mending sample. Unfinished at the bottom are a few random letters. The text is bleak.

"My Grave And Coffin Are At Hand My Glass Hath Run." It was kept with care.

Elizabeth Kempton, 1843, a poor girl at home.
Struggling with literacy. The peacock is not the usual English one, but one more often found on samplers from the border counties or Scotland.

Chapter 7
PLAIN SEWING & CLOTHING SAMPLERS

"The lot of saints hath been
Afflictions, wants and scorns,
For Hee that was the best of men
Was mockt and crowned with thorns.

God give me wisdom to direct my waes;
I ask not riches nor yet length of daes.

Delight in learning soon doth bring
A child to learn the hardest thing.
The sampler of Anne Thruckstone, 1723.

When Victoria came to the throne in 1837, free schools for the poor were increasingly available, but few learned to master pen and ink. If poor girls wrote at all it was with slate-pencils on slates as boys did. Needlework lessons depended on families who had subscribed to build the school. Lady volunteers taught needlework, bringing materials from their own homes for the girls to work. Without that help the teaching of the subject would have been impossible in many schools, and the ladies brought better cloth and better thread than the children or the school could afford. With it, they learned a skill useful in any home and a qualification for employment.

The Plain-Sewing Needlework of Poor Schools was gathered and kept to prove the competence of their instruction. Those practical works are scarcely recognised as Samplers, and sewn verses are very rare. This was the baggage that charity and deference imposed on needlework.

An early Needlework Manual of Instruction from the British and Foreign Schools Society Institution at Colraine, Ireland was copied in stitches on linen sheets. Many women used their needles for correspondence as the only reliable writing instrument they had.

Mondays, Wednesdays and Fridays. Assemble 10 o'clock.
The children form semi-circles and read from the lesson given them by the general monitor.
The list of names called over, and the monitors take account of the absentees.
The reading monitors question the classes on what they have been reading.
The reading monitors hear their classes spell the most difficult words in their reading lessons.

Another duty of the monitors was to
Call over the names of the good and bad girls who are rewarded and punished accordingly.

There follows a timetable of Religious Instruction, Arithmetic, and tests on what the children had learned. Then comes what the girls were taught in Needlework. The first class included threading the needle and making plain running and back stitches

Second Class	*1st Division*	*a zig-zag tacking stitch.*
	2nd Division	*hemming.*

Fourth Class		*bands on a gathered cuff*
Fifth Class		*button holes.*
Sixth Class		*button making.*
Seventh Class,	*First Division*	*coloured borders in large figure 8.*
	2nd. Division	*Cross-stitch borders.*
Eighth Class		*a tiny darning sampler. (Wool darns not the Damascus linen)*
Ninth Class		*a gathered frill edging.*
Tenth Class		*an alphabet sampler.*

By 1834, Workhouse Unions were teaching poor children to read as well as other profitable skills. Since part of the cost was carried by the Poor Rate, Schools of Industry could balance marketable skills with literacy. The worst were all that Dickens could imagine; drab neglect and unfeeling squalor. The best did produce samplers, and their curriculum was absorbed into the "British" and "National" schools.

Two years after Queen Victoria came to the throne, these two voluntary societies published new programmes of Needlework. Government, having made the first grants to Poor Schools, encouraged its own standards for provision and teaching.

The British and National systems of teaching drew on long practise in poor schools of earlier times. Plain-sewing Samplers were designed to discipline poor children to patient industriousness; making and mending household linen.

Teaching Manuals left unprinted spaces at the end of every chapter, where examples of the expected work, on small squares of cloth, were sewn onto the pages. This ensured some uniformity of teaching and standards.

Lessons on tacking, running stitch, seams, hemming, blanket-stitch and buttonhole produced samples two or three inches square. Pupils were expected to sew each sample into an exercise book, copying their learning into albums, just as richer children made their copybooks in Writing or their Cyphering books in Arithmetic.

Poor girls learned to put frills and gussets onto cloth. They patched worn holes invisibly by inserting a square of the material first with plain, then with patterned cloth. When they were able to make their stitches regular and small, they worked miniature garments in cotton cloth, incorporating all the skills they had mastered. Such baby caps, pinafores, dresses, and gentlemen's shirts with tiny buttonholes, were the samplers of the poor. Some were later raided to dress dolls, but some survive as they were made, kept as a memorial to demanding days.

The syllabus copied traditional needlework of the best 18th century orphanages and poor schools. There was nothing new, but what was before rare advanced to bring needlework skill within reach of most girls. The tiny garments that were part of the syllabus were like the Baby Linen offered by the pupils of Cheltenham Female Orphan Asylum. Whatever rules society imposes, schools copy good practices that have shown success in other schools. Imposition can avoid bad schools; but leadership and emulation usually produce the best.

Knitting with wool was taught, and the art of wool darning. The curriculum was so uniform that any two surviving plain-sewing sample-books are remarkably similar. Schools in affluent districts allowed more generous details. Toward the end of the curriculum the girls made an Alphabet Sampler. Wool thread was sewn on a square of wide-meshed canvas seldom more than six inches in size. Often letters were sewn only in the capitals young maids in service would use to mark their employer's linen.

Modesty permitted the girl's initials in the sampler, or a full name, and even an emblem or two. Perhaps a date was sewn in a sampler rather larger in size. With few exceptions only one colour, black, red or blue, was permitted.

If any embroidery emblems were allowed, they were an extravagance of that particular school, contrary to the spirit of the teaching manuals. Usually they did not include the verses traditional in English Embroidery samplers. So they contained neither the aspirations of richer samplers nor the subservient pleas of the Charity Schools. For girls not destined for domestic service, needlework gave a valuable skill, serviceable for busy housewives; but art and personality were considered of no account at all.

National examinations and qualifications were unknown. Needlework albums and Alphabet Samplers were certificates of merit to show prospective employers. The most charming of these exercises incorporated the lessons of the curriculum in miniature clothes. The smocks had their tucks and pockets, and in the front a tiny patch of "invisible" mending or darning. These mean, plain exercises show the care of poor girls at school. Colraine called their exercise "samplers", and though some collectors disdain the title, they run alongside the history of grander samplers made in schools and homes of richer families.

As soon as any school in its generosity allowed girls to do more than the manual allowed, they rushed to make the more familiar kind of sampler, with its emblems, its verses and its yearning for art and perfection.

The reign of Victoria was a time of immense social advancement. Skilled artisans improved their standard of life and their finances. Before the end of her reign, Council Schools, as they were then called, contained children whose talents and ambitions would lead them into new social opportunities. Alongside them sat other children whose poverty was ingrained as the dirt on their unshod feet. When samplers show a cursive alphabet, it is a sign the girls were taught to write as well as read.

A plain alphabet sampler was in one school the most that any girl could attempt. In another, emblems, the name of the school, a flowering border and an alphabet in script letters show something similar to the expectations of private schools.

The early English and American tradition of "Baby Showering" was an occasion when family and friends of a new mother gathered to show their common love and hope in gifts to the new-born. It was a tradition of adults, and children too; and it is a joy and privilege still expressed. On one piece of baby linen made in 1763 an insert of Holie-point lace forms words that are so like the sentiments of a sampler:

Sarah Everard Workt   *Fear God And*
This Baby Linen 1763   *Keep His Laws*

Holie-point lace was a skill beyond the reach of childhood but for rare exceptions in 17th century samplers. From a short revival in the 18th century also comes a tiny pair of infant socks sewn on No. 24 needles with a texture like gossamer covered with the most beautiful frost-like patterns.

Such unrestrained devotion makes one wonder at the delicacy, great love, and awe that a new birth can bring forth; a universal hope for perfection, and reverence for what is pure and innocent. Historians have rightly insisted that we should know how smelly, flea-ridden, coarse and selfish the western world was in the past: but these needle-works are visible proof that care, cleanliness, selfless love, and duty were also part of those times, and found in ordinary lives.

Such beauty was not made to be carelessly worn, soiled and discarded; but to be washed and kept, and worn out by generations of love. We cannot be sure which were worked by young girls, nor can they be called samplers with any great assurance; but the early Victorian Poor-Schools were aware of this tradition in forming their needlework syllabuses. We know exactly how children made the examples of plain work wrought in Poor Schools, and they deserve to be valued as Samplers of patient, traditional needlework.

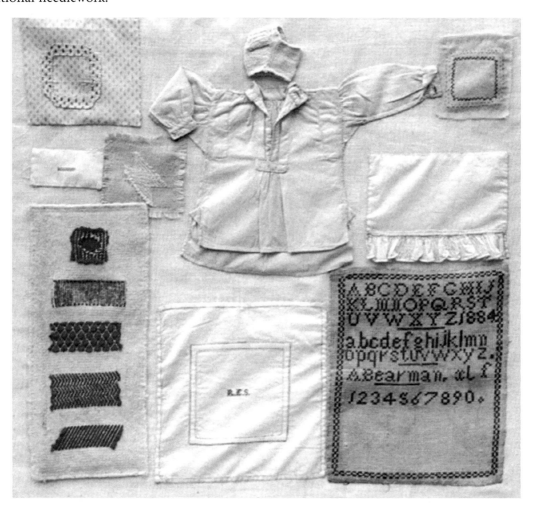

Plain-sewing course-work and Alphabet Sampler. Annie Bearman, Baldock National Girls' School, 1887.

Adult needlework is seldom signed, let alone dated, and it does not show the age of the woman who wrought it. The vanity this would have implied was excused in Samplers because they were tasks with a beginning, a single purpose and an end; and because they were often gifts in memory of childhood. They were a child's delight to please and a parent's pride in that accomplishment.

Needlework becomes a Sampler, whether from the 17th or 19th century, by its traditional purpose. A piece of Berlin wool-work that includes a name, a date and an age, even without the alphabet, would be the work of a child, and stood in the place of a Sampler. It is entitled to the name. The tiny garments of the poor school syllabus are Samplers. Baby Linen, seat covers, needlework pictures and fire-screens sewn by adults are not. Samplers less often celebrate the beginning of childhood, than the imminence of its ending.

Before the making of children's samplers came to its own end, a sentimental wish for survival led the poor to use cards punched with small, regular holes. Echoes of past sampler traditions were sewn onto them in tent or cross-stitch. They were cheap and easy attempts to perpetuate old ways. As mementoes of childhood, they did not require the skill and patience that gave pride to recollection of the past. By 1918 samplers were seldom made; either by the rich or by the poor. The traditions had died, at home or in schools.

While samplers had been an important element in the childhood of girls, it is amazing what patient skill formed the variety of stitches in the work of comfortable families. Their imagination is stunning, and the honour of the work persuaded some girls to make their sampler while very young. If the invention of a sampler made by a seven-year-old shows less imagination, the dedication and patience of the work can be incredible to an age that asks so much less of children.

It was the verses on English samplers which best expressed the ideals of their time; what was most admired and what faults disfigured perfection. When those ideals of character were markedly different for the poor than they were for the rich, and when they were remarkably different for women than for men, ideals became a trap, often tender, sometimes cruel.

Annie Bearman's Smock.
A compendium of all she had learned in Needlework

English State Schools; History, Structure and Title, 1802 - 1902.

England never initiated a centrally administered Education System for its common people, as the Americans, Dutch, Germans, French and Scots had done. The quality of English school buildings and lessons varied enormously. An adventurous head-teacher, with affluent well-educated parents as immediate neighbours, and a gifted Needlework teacher, could produce exceptional standards.

Understanding Victorian Schools is obscured by a complication of management and intention. The history of English Poor Schools is a story of successive failures and dying hopes to provide reliable and generous teaching. Yet the persistent need for literacy grew ever more urgent; demanding new costs and new solutions in each generation. The intentions and trials involve changes of title that are themselves confusing. In the course of the 19th century, the work of church charities in schooling the poor was supported and then overtaken by the intervention of government agencies.

The sampler of Louisa Jane Carswell, Dover Charity School, 1846.
Courtesy of Jean Panter, Woodstock.

A hundred years after Louisa sewed this sampler, merit and the uneven effects of poverty still hovered over opportunity that state school pupils could rise to their potential. Louisa sewed it to prove her worth as a servant in a grander home than her own. Her work is evidence of a step on the long trek to better opportunities.

The history of her school stands remarkably as an example of changes that transformed English Poor Schools into State Schools.

In 1616 a school was founded in one of the old ecclesiastical buildings between Dover Market Place and Queen Street. Titles of such schools usually named the benefactor, but this school for the education of six poor children was founded by Dover Corporation and was known as Udney Charity School after its first master, Robert Udney.

That hall was closed in 1628 but similar charity provision by local worthies continued its purposes elsewhere on renewed foundations. The Society for the Promulgation of Christian Knowledge is not likely to have ignored Dover unless it was believed the town already had provision for the teaching of poor children. The rise and fall of the 18th century Charity School movement has already been explained.

In 1787, at last, the SPCK founded a school for 45 boys and 35 girls which they considered a continuation of the old Foundation. In Queen Street, "Dover Charity School" became a title rather than a description. It was supported by annual voluntary subscriptions from wealthy parishioners, augmented by regular Church of England charity sermons.

Between 1802 and 1902 there were at least six separate developments that ended in the construction of state elementary schools. At the beginning, government had no part in building or providing education for the poor. That was left to two Voluntary Societies; The British and Foreign Schools Society was non-denominational, The National Society for the Education of the Poor taught the precepts of the Church of England.

"British Schools" and "National Schools" had been inspired by one alarming problem and a single hope for its solution; the urban poor and the Monitorial Principle.

At the beginning of the 19th century, the Charity School movement was in decline, and few older attempts at schooling the poor had survived. The wretched lives of helpless poverty could be more or less hidden in village life, and more or less helped by personal charity. But London and the vast new towns of the industrial revolution swarmed beyond control with untaught and vulnerable children.

They invaded the consciences of comfortable families. Their begging, their demanding, the language and habits of wild, reckless gangs, their uniform dirty, shabby, dangerous and useless lives were a reproach and a menace to affluent people who walked the same streets. Poor children needed the disciplines of a school; but the costs were daunting.

In the country, Rates were only paid by the gentry, by farmers and propertied tradesmen. They were spent on highways, market control, doles to poor families, and workhouses for those who would not or could not help themselves. No one wanted to pay more. Rates were not used for education until 1870 and even then were avoided by most communities until the last years of the century. Charity donation by churches was the customary funding for schools, but teacher salaries were too much of a burden even after school buildings had been subscribed and built.

A Quaker, ex-soldier, Joseph Lancaster was the first to demonstrate a complete solution; a method whereby one teacher could teach hundreds of children.

The Monitorial idea was that up to three hundred children, (*he claimed a thousand, but did not demonstrate that*) in a vast hall, furnished with forms for the infants and desks for the over sevens, would all be under the eye of one teacher. The seeming impossibility was made plausible by two principles; complete obedience, and the use of older pupils as Monitors.

After Lancaster had addressed his great hall of children to emphasise their duties, Monitors, like corporals in the army, took his orders and went to teach stations of pupils those things they had learned. The senior monitors stood at the row ends calling out questions of English or Arithmetic and responding with praise or blame for the children who stood to show answers on their slates. Meanwhile junior monitors gathered smaller groups into the side aisles. Classes stood about the monitor in a semi-circle while he asked them one by one to attempt a piece of mental arithmetic, to spell a word, to name a county town or the longest river in the world. The method required no books.

The system was based on military discipline, with orders and responses barked out. A similar drill had enabled British regiments, amid the roar of muskets and canon, to fire one ball a minute more than any French regiment they faced. Monitors taught what they knew almost entirely by repetition and memory. The process was a pandemonium of noise with the disciplines of a battlefield.

Soon it was found that the extraordinary authority of those who first developed the idea was impossible to find among general teacher recruits. Obviously, writing with pen and ink, or needlework and many possible lessons could not be taught this way; but at least the children were under control, and learning good and useful lessons rather than the delinquencies of the streets.

Lancaster's School in the Borough Road was visited by fashionable gentry. The royal family supported him enthusiastically and George III declared his hope that every child in his kingdom might be taught to read. New schools were opened and girls were admitted. Piqued by the admiration shown to Lancaster, the Church of England drew attention to their own Andrew Bell who had run a school based on similar principles for Indian Army children overseas. A National Society was formed and their Monitorial Schools, opened for families of Anglican congregations, taught only the forms and principles of that church.

Soon afterwards Lancaster was involved in a scandal, to do with the indulgent privileges of his monitors, some dubious methods of punishment, and financial irregularity. He fled the kingdom and was welcomed in America. The impetus of his ideas continued under a newly formed society, The British and Foreign Schools Society.

The "British" schools it opened in this and many other countries gave no religious instruction for they served Christians who were Presbyterians, Baptists, Methodists, Congregationalists, Quakers, Catholics etc., and Jews or Humanists, all of them excluded from "National" Schools.

There was fierce competition, animosity even, between the two Societies.

Monitorial Schools were formed by local subscription, so they responded to local variation in detail. Generally "British Schools" were more likely to be free, to teach boys and girls together for many lessons, and to consider writing early and quickly on the slate to be important in schooling. For Singing, Needlework, Geography and other lessons, classes were sent from the great hall to a raised gallery at one end. "National Schools" were more likely to divide the school into Boys' and Girls' departments by a partition that separated the children except for special occasions. More often they charged a penny a week, and asked an additional penny for the brighter pupils to advance in pen and ink writing. Copybooks of precise cursive script were the dominating tradition of private schools, and slowly these and other text books entered the Poor Schools.

Text books, when they came, were long lists of questions and answers; the facts that children had to learn by heart. Knowledge was largely an accumulation of memory.

In 1816 Parliament set up a Select Committee on the Education of the Lower Orders, and for nearly twenty years they debated how much help they could or ought to offer these new schemes for teaching the poor. In 1820, Dover Charity School was rebuilt to house 200 boys and 200 girls, financed by contributions from St Mary's parish.

Teacher training did not exist, but if it had, it could never make common what was practically extraordinary. Failure meant that the economies promised did not arise, yet the large schools now existed and the evident need had to be met somehow.

Assistant teachers were employed to take divisional classes in schools much above a hundred pupils; and one or two school leavers were employed at pocket-money wages as pupil-teachers to help test smaller groups. Pupil-teachers were often inspired by the spirit of learning, but Elementary lessons allowed the poor were little beyond Reading Writing and Arithmetic, so the greater world of knowledge was only available to those who picked it up by contact with the School Teacher in times they were not themselves teaching.

In the second half of the century, that system was rescued from failure by giving the best pupil-teachers scholarships to Teacher Training Colleges. In this manner many bright young people, eager for learning, found their way from poverty to lowly-paid respectability.

By 1834, government grants from a successor Select Committee of the Privy Council for the Education of the Poor began to aid voluntary societies with capital costs in building Poor Schools.

In 1846 the school hall at Dover would have been divided into two by a partition; the girls and infants on one side with a lady assistant teacher nominally under the control of the Master. The Master taught his boys on the other side, and the Girls' side wished he had more control over them. They disturbed lessons with their boisterous noise, and outside they shouted rude things when the girls had to go to the earth-closet.

By this time, the Education Committee of Parliament printed advice on methods and contents of teaching. A system of government inspection began to draw together the great variety of standards that arose from the local nature of Voluntary Schools. Teachers were employed without certification and with little or perhaps great talents and understanding. Their character, patience and pay were similarly diverse.

By 1862 national government had largely accepted the need to pay teachers, to inspect teaching, to control what was taught and to set standards of acceptability. The school tasks were divided into Standards, and though standard three and four might be taught together, three and five might required separate classes within the one room.

The second Reform Act of 1867 entitled almost every man in the kingdom to vote. The more intelligent of the gentry, shocked to realise their old privilege had passed over to the masses, decide that they must now "educate their masters." The wholly illiterate were attended to, but the standards were not extravagant. Most pupils left school round about eleven years of age, and Standard Seven, the top, was reached by very few. Those who reached a fair standard of elementary education by eleven could leave school and start to earn a living.

In villages not yet provided with schools by the National or British Societies, an act of 1870 began erection of free schools financed from a rate on households. These in-fillers were managed by locally created School Boards, and were known as Board Schools. To prevent an imposition of such rates upon their householders, many towns agreed to end the penny or twopence a week that had until then been asked of their poor scholars.

Soon all Poor Schools became virtually free.

In the same year, the boys' and girls' schools at Dover went their separate ways. Dover Charity School in Queen Street was no longer large enough for the need, and it was reopened, for 572 boys, managed by the National Society and financed from public funds through Dover Education

Committee. It was now named St. Mary's National School (Boys). The Girls and the Infants were accommodated in new buildings elsewhere.

Few state systems in other countries would have allowed the mixture of Boys', Girls' and Co-educational Schools to grow. It is a feature of English schools because the state came so late in the establishment of Poor Schools.

When County Councils were established in 1888, their Education Committees were given the task of managing Poor Schools. It was no longer possible for towns to avoid the cost of education on local rates. Today education is by far the greatest of all their costs.

The few schools that preferred to be managed by the old Voluntary Societies were supervised by the County Councils. The work of the British and National Societies, in creating schools for all, was done. Many poor schools were re-named Council Schools and the title Poor School was already a misnomer; for the not-so-poor were now happy to send their children to schools run by the state.

In 1902, for the first time, County Councils were allowed to build and finance Secondary Schools on the rates. The school in Queen's Street was known as a Public Elementary School. It took another generation before Public Secondary Schools became common, but in time the old Charity School building came to be called St. Mary's Church of England Primary School. It was now co-educational again and called a Junior School to distinguish it from the Infants' School.

Schools founded in Victorian times show their origins in their names. 'National' schools were named after the parish church even if built far from it. E.g. St Mary's, Baldock. 'British' schools served many chapels and meeting houses, and were named from their location. E.g. Pond Lane School, Baldock; or Queen's Street School, Hitchin.

Elleanor Johnson's sampler from Wearmouth National School. 1846

Eliza Tabitha Carr, Bratton British School, 1865.
Proudly wrought by a fourteen year old; later neglected.

Eliza Tabitha Carr's sampler is unusually ornamental for a "Poor School" sampler. It might almost have been made in a private academy for well-to-do girls. It shows her patience and the encouragement of her school. Eliza sewed it aged fourteen, probably as a monitor or Pupil-teacher, helping with the youngsters, reluctant to leave school while the call of learning urged her on. Needlework was her favourite subject but surely not the only one that led her from poverty to a world of knowledge.

Her needlework teacher, Mrs Porter, (*called the sempstress in the school log book*) was ill. Eliza applied for the vacant post but the headmaster's mother was preferred. In two years the headmaster and his mother left. It was probably then that Eliza was given the post, and she may have under-studied it in the meantime. We do know she resigned as sempstress of Bratton School in 1876, and it is a sensible guess to think she did so when she married.

Social advancement is seldom easy. Eliza was a keen and talented child, and Bratton British School had the quality to make a ladder for her hopes.

The dying end to a belief that the majority of any population was inherently and divinely set to be non-academic, dull and obedient is not relevant to the history of Samplers. The inspiration to sew them, having languished long, expired in the early years of the twentieth century.

Women at home filled the impatient hours of the Great War with proud and confident needlework; mementoes embroidered on cushions and heartfelt gifts. They arrive today in dusty salerooms, too sad and sorry to be valued with the hopes that inspired them.

The 1914 - 18 battles on the Western Front did not end needlework, but the generation of widows and spinsters left behind by the carnage lost their heart for samplers. For the rich, embroidery was too slight and subservient; other ambitions inflamed them. For the poor, the servile cast of plain-sewing did not match the pride and sad determination that flowed. Both continued to use dressmaking needlework to proclaim their independence, their serviceability, and their love of fashion.

Whatever and how improvements came afterward to the State System of Schooling, the age of needlework samplers for children had ended, in schools and in the home.

By the time Tabitha made her sampler at Bratton School the yearning was beginning to fade. Young ladies gave up making samplers when the poor began to copy them. In the emerging state schools, an Alphabet Sampler was neither art nor joy. It was a certificate of skill, and whether the girl needed it to go into service or not, it was done with the same dutiful care she did all her lessons; because most girls are like that.

The Manners and Disciplines of 19th Century Poor Schools

Infants sat at the front on "forms", and at the very back were desks for a few Writing pupils learning to copy the English Round Hand with pen and ink. They, and those given "Silent Reading" tasks, were the only pupils not waiting for orders, waving their hands wildly in hope to be asked a question, or crying out answers to the catechisms.

Classes alternated between tense anticipation, furious activity, and long periods of silence and stillness. To relax the stiffness of long attention, physical training was begun. In the whole barn-like building, children, sitting or standing where they were, followed orders to stretch their arms and bend their legs and bodies. Some did it with wooden dumbbells they were given to hold.

Whatever the lesson, if not encouraged to speak, the children were to observe absolute silence. For breach of the rule, the whole class would cease lessons and sit upright and still with hands on their heads, frozen in silence until the teacher thought they deserved to relax. For inattention or error, the cane or tawse (for girls) was used frequently. The children held out their palms to receive the stinging punishment. Long, persistent intellectual dullness or carelessness was punished by bringing the child out before the school. Offenders stood on a stool or in the corner, publicly reprimanded and humiliated as a dunce.

Disobedience was more serious. Girls were seldom asked to bend over, as recalcitrant boys did in front of the school. The two or three whacks they got on their back-sides from the master's cane mixed pain with humiliation. It tested a boy's stoic character, and it certainly impressed the companions who witnessed it.

Needlework classes were usually worked at tables, and often taught by an instructress not a teacher. Those to be tested at "reading with expression" waited in line to be heard by the teacher. Those chanting or singing out responses to music, or lessons learned by heart, were taught as a "class".

The Head of a School was usually a Master, and a senior woman assistant came to be given special care of the girls and infants. Where two "Schools" were partitioned off, the mistress began to achieve some independence, and school log-books illustrate how different custom could be.

Imagine such a school-room in the 1880's, lit by oil lamp or gas; no playground and just space outside for boys and girls to go to the lavatories. They were newly installed with running water and sewage drains because the cholera scare of the 1860's had wakened the nation to environmental health.

The "Schoolmaster", Mr. Lloyd, persuaded a farmer to let the boys play football on an adjacent field, formed a team, coached it, and made it win. He took the keen boys for nature walks on Saturdays; brought them back to rehearse a play in evenings; and made all of them attend briskly and cheerfully to lively classroom lessons. He brought local celebrities to the school who could tell the boys of marvellous sciences, bold responsibilities, and distant lands.

Most of all he chased up parents of absent boys, demanding written explanations and shaming local shopkeepers, even those who were managers of his school, to send their errand boys in time for school. He made sure farmers returned their labourers to school at harvest's end as soon as the school year began. Within a year of his coming to the school, the boys had the highest attendance in the county.

Mr Lloyd made them proud and gave them dignity. He used the cane freely and was determined every one of his boys should come to school and learn as hard as they could. Parents were glad enough to discover someone who would knock the wildness out of their boys, and the boys themselves were cheerfully employable in work that demanded literacy and initiative.

Miss Turner, of the Girls' department, was glad of his authority when dramatic or musical entertainments were organised that required voluntary participation by boys and girls together. The whole town bought tickets and rejoiced at the talents of their children. Mr Lloyd and Miss Turner shared a pride in their school, but her manner with her girls was of a different nature to his with his boys.

Girls without interest in school only disturbed the willing, eager girls, and there were plenty of those. Miss Turner fought with no-one, and left her male managers to chase up parents and employers of truants, knowing they would shirk the trouble. She let parents and her pupils know that if they did not have the commitment due to learning they would not be welcome when they did want to come. Rightly, she recognised that truants do not want to stay away from school so much as come just when it pleases them.

Miss Turner gave her whole energy to the willing girls, teaching them well and leading them into lady-like manners and courtesies. They were quiet, obedient, and modestly sure of themselves.

Life's opportunities were restricted for the poor and more so for women, but her girls left school with more knowledge and social judgement than most. When the school was so much to the purpose of striving families, new pupils joined the school faster than truants faded away. Her school was full, and desperate families found their places taken when they discovered what non-attendance had cost them.

In their own ways, Mr Lloyd and Miss Turner both ran much better schools than average. The difference was simply that the Boys' School was improved by discipline, good teaching and natural emulation; the Girls' by good teaching, emulation and a gentle discipline. In both it became a privilege to belong; to a school that raised expectations, and for a nation to be proud of. In the eighties, pride in the nation and empire flourished.

All Victorian Poor Schools faced a persistent problem with non-attendance and truancy. When father was absent, ill or only fitfully at work, mother would take in washing and slave to put food on the table. When mother was ill or over-pressed with other people's laundry, she would have great need of her daughter's help at home; to go errands, to look after the sick or the younger children, to cook and clean. If a boy could earn pennies as a tradesman's mate or on casual engagement hunting golf balls for one of the gentry, the family need might be urgent. Going to school took second place in the order of things.

Truants absent because they disliked lessons, the teacher, or exposure to the sneers of richer and cleverer companions added to the problem. Occasional Church Feasts and outings, with the sanctions of piety, were hard to refuse; and annual fetes or the visit of the circus to town were temptations that fought against the growth of loyalty and commitment to school. Some children knew that family influence, a strong body and willingness to learn were better guarantees of employment than anything they learnt in school lessons.

Ill-attendance broke the continuity of lessons, and picking up was difficult as well as disturbing for others in the class. Girls were tempted by the chance to earn money spinning, or plaiting straw for the market in straw hats. Businessmen set up little factories for infants and called them schools to pretend they were places for children to learn anything except what profited the business.

The harvest often closed schools because whole families were out in the fields as long as the light lasted. Gleaning for poor girls, and man's work for the boys was a time honoured tradition, as strong and ancient as the land. Old customs were hard to break.

Other causes than casual truancy contributed to bad attendance at school. Infections ran through the streets of rich and poor without the checks we expect today. Whooping cough, measles, cholera, scarlet-fever, pneumonia, croup and influenza would cut attendance at school from the 160 ordinarily to perhaps twenty. The school would be entirely closed for some time each year to prevent more children catching whatever plague it was that harassed them.

Social habit condemned many girls to a life of dirt and disease repugnant to others however much the fault was not of the girls' own making. One school's log book mentions a girl "with clothing so offensive that no child could sit near her, and she was sent home to be made sweeter". There was no gentle way to hide the humiliation. Ringworm disfigured the face and scalp, and the advised cure was to pull hairs one by one with tweezers out of suppurating sores. Mrs Beeton's Household Management advised the "daily application of Whitfield's Ointment or Iodine.

They were ill-nourished. Poor wretches to be so outcast, disfigured and tortured!

It was common for children to have no coats and many went barefoot. In winter storms, fingers turned blue, then swelled to chilblains that stung and burst into sores. Walking barefoot through snow-covered streets, until the end of the century, poor children arrived at school frozen and unable to walk further. White-boned fingers were thrust into laps or into the mouth, slowly coaxing circulation back into frozen limbs.

The "Poor" is a wide description that covers many grades of struggling hope and spiritual degradation. The family history of Louisa Jane Carswell helps us to estimate where she, the girl behind the sampler, was placed in the ranks of poverty.

Louisa was baptised at St Mary's Church, Dover on 23rd of October 1833 having been born on 22nd September to John Arthur and Ann Carswell in the same year. Her father, 21 at the time, was an agricultural labourer. Poor certainly; but there was a great distance between those with steady employment and reputation and those liable to be dismissed with each change of fortune that hit farming.

Louisa had eight sisters and two brothers. Four of them died in infancy, a record of mortality no worse than average which does not argue neglect or extreme poverty. Her elder sister was a servant to a richer family in the same street, and a younger sister later lived as an unmarried servant to Baroness Embling of Essex who lived in a grand Dover house.

The influence of the baroness probably helped John Arthur to a steadier job as Sexton, for he named another daughter Embling, and they moved to tied accommodation in a large new cemetery. All in all, it argues for his standing in the community as a man of respect and reliability.
Raising crops was an uncertain occupation, but those who buried the dead were never out of work.

The forties were hard times. The slow, steady advance in prosperity of the respectable poor during Victoria's reign is less reported than the spectacular crimes of its villains and the plight of its desperate poor. Burial records show that Ann Marks Carswell, clearly the mother of Louisa Jane, died in 1902 aged 92. Born five years before the Battle of Waterloo, she died at the Workhouse in Union Lane, Dover. She might well have out-lived her husband and all her children. Ann would have known joy, grief and pride, but ended her days alone and abandoned.

Truancy in Poor Schools was a problem that continued throughout Victoria's reign. Governments tried to condition their grants to the pupils' attendance, but systematic cheating blunted its effectiveness. Compulsion was tried but could seldom be enforced against the waywardness of some families and the urgent need private gentry and businesses had for child labour. Reward schemes and medals had more effect, but provision and quality of individual teachers was patchy all over the country. The saving grace came slowly as the pay, the conditions and the understanding of the poor advanced.

State Elementary Schools taught eighty percent of the population at the end of the century. When their old boys joined army ranks as volunteers for the Boer War, their average height was five inches shorter than officers who had been taught at Public School. This discrepancy indicates the difference in health between the affluent and the relatively poor, and it was still clearly visible in recruits to the Great War. What shocked the nation was the physical unfitness of their state-schooled men.

Where they could be, playgrounds were constructed round elementary schools so children could drill, exercise and play outside.

There were better schools before that date and worse schools after it. Between the child and the teacher, such a variety of good and bad things can make schooldays wonderful or frustrating. We must live with a variety of good and bad schools, and rich and poor, or fashions and facilities, or the errors of times past and the wisdoms of the present will not march us on unerringly to make childhood happy. The Golden Rule is as true today as it was in 1860 when Emma Barrett sewed her Text Sampler in a common school:

> *To do to others as I would*
> *That they should do to me.*
> *Will make me honest kind and good*
> *As children ought to be.*

A simple Aphabet Sampler 1822.
Selina Wise made it generously and thoroughly enough to show she was not very poor, but that the school where she was taught was very good.

Chapter 8
DELIGHT, DUTY, or DRUDGERY?

"Industrious ingenuity may find
Noble employment for the female mind"
Hannah Butler's sampler, 1812, aged 13.

Whether samplers were made at home or in school, the character of the work is inseparable from the spirit in which it was done. Consider what evidence we have from history or from the work itself to tell us how much was enforced social conditioning, how much an accepted part of natural life, and how much was a joyous gift of life itself.

In some things, custom binds us tighter than the law. Needlework had been among the customary duties of women from the dawn of human existence. Needles survive from the Stone Age to prove the existence of threads that have not. Domestic sewing was artistically depicted before histories of its use, and it was then in the hands of women. Art and anthropology argue for a custom of immeasurable antiquity.

Among the rich, when necessity was no longer the cause, women took up embroidery as a token of their patient love. They rejoiced in it. Most of them did not merely endure what could not be changed; they took pride in their artistry. They put off plain-sewing to their servants, knowing it well enough to be able to instruct and criticise the work.

Servant girls had too much of it; but what made it a chore, was not the work itself, but that it was done for the linen of another household than their own. Those who were neither servants nor employers of servants, found it one of the kindest of their duties, and one that could be done demurely and companionably. It was a domestic skill more than a labour. Washing and cleaning were simply chores that had to be done, and if so, done with care. Cooking and bringing up children were matters of domestic pride; but too hectic, demanding and onerous to have the calm appeal of the sewing circle.

Such generalizations ignore individuals who may have loved, taken pride in, or hated any one of these duties. Samplers, when they came to be the mark of young ladies, also became objects of affection for poorer girls who could not afford extravagant linens and silks, and had to contain their efforts within humbler bounds.

Few samplers would have been made without some sense of personal obligation; to be patient, careful and praiseworthy. It was the expected thing in gentle homes. The slow and disciplined task allowed opportunities for grudging girls to spoil their work; but the quality proves that nearly all samplers were taken up with love, and finished with satisfaction. The best works predominate among those that survive, but they survive remarkably.

It is recorded in schools that to be allowed to begin a sampler was regarded as a treat. In Ackworth, even such plain and painstaking work as a darning sampler was sought eagerly and worked with pride.

The sampler was a personal and visible testament to ability. Its place as ritual in the coming of age meant that the work celebrated personal identity.

If there were girls who hated their samplers, it was because the whole of their needlework was a crashing bore, and an unjust imposition placed like the manacles of slavery on womankind. Such ideas could only breed among the liberal rich. Needlework had to be done; by whom if not by women? If it was an imposition, the fault was blamed on Eve, and women mostly responded by doing their work with the same conscientious pride as men bore their allotted burdens.

Yet some girls smarted under the assumption of women's subordination to men. Samplers were meant to be safe and decorative, not self-important. Most verses were conventional, with an implied impropriety of independent thought; but they challenged a few families to choose bolder themes. The acquiescent and limited range of many English sampler verses, dramatically contrast with the bold aphorisms composed for the boys' copybooks. These infiltrated girls' copybooks, and crept into some samplers.

At school, the girls would be at their needles when the boys were struggling with more intellectually demanding studies, or engaged in any one of the hundred idiotic things boys do when let free. Some girls would have been glad, some smug, and some seething with envy.

Samplers show that most girls accepted what every authority told them was unchangeable; that to achieve respect they must seek different and humbler virtues than those expected of boys. Sometimes this argument was expressed through a particular skill, as if the pen was as inappropriate in the hands of a woman as the needle in the hands of a man. More often, sampler verse struck a balance, but some assumed women should not compete outside the home, and there be subject to father or husband. In 1830, Jane Bailey expressed in her sampler this more general acceptance of a woman's place:

> *"Seek to be good, but aim not to be great;*
> *A woman's noblest station is retreat.*
> *Her fairest virtues fly from public sight;*
> *Domestic worth still shuns too strong a light."*

This resignation makes exceptions to it a delight to find. A rare adventurous spirit entered some sampler verse; and in some households a more generous expectation was growing in the eighteenth century.

> *"To my best, my friends are free,*
> *Free with that, and free with me,*
> *Free to pass the harmless joke,*
> *And the tube sedately smoke,*
> *Free to drink just what they please,*
> *As at home and at their ease,*
> *Free to stay a night or so,*
> *When uneasy, free to go."*
>
> Mary Dale's sampler, Drayton School, 1798.

The placid and obedient occupation of Reading was recommended for all women, but Writing, which so easily slipped into opinion, was a subject needing justification.

"Ye springing fair, whose virtuous minds incline
To all that's curious, innocent and fine,
With admiration in your works we read
The various textures of the twining thread;
Then let your fingers, whose unrival'd skill
Exalts the needle, grace the noble quill.
An artless scrawl the blushing scribbler shames;
All should be fair that virtuous woman frames".

Frances Woods' sampler, 1784.

A desire to be free to write and publish, to travel riding astride the horse, to smoke cigars, and to learn mathematics like the boys rather than the simple arithmetic of household use; all these and other yearnings interrupted the quiet concentration of girls at their samplers: but only rich and educated girls could hope to be free of the needle.

In 1714 a curious piece appeared in the "Spectator". It complained of two nieces who go to bed tired of doing nothing, and of hours *"thrown away in dress, play, visits, and the like"* which in the past *"were employed writing out receipts* (what we would call recipes) *or working beds, chairs, and hangings for the family. …….. It grieves my heart to see a couple of proud idle flirts sipping their tea, for a whole afternoon, in a room hung round with the industry of their great-grandmother."*

The Spectator's rejoinder was full of lofty ideals and patronising admonitions to the bright young things of the day:

"What a delightful entertainment must it be to the fair sex, whom their native modesty, and the tenderness of men towards them, exempts from public business, to pass their hours in imitating fruits and flowers, raising a new creation in their closets, walking among the shades and groves planted by themselves, in surveying heroes slain by their needle, or little Cupids which they have brought into the word without pain!"

"I cannot forbear wishing, that several writers of that sex had chosen to apply themselves rather to tapestry than rhime. Your pastoral poetesses may vent their fancy in rural landskips, and place despairing shepherds under silken willows, or drown them in a stream of mohair. (If) any pretty creature is void of genius, I must nevertheless insist upon her working, if it be only to keep her out of harm's way … because it takes them off from scandal, the usual attendant of teatables, and all other unactive scenes of life. While they are forming their birds and beasts, their neighbours will be allowed to be the fathers of their own children."

The common enough masculine conceit of disparaging women authors, was probably meant to provoke. Three issues later, back came the reply:-

"Mr. Spectator,

The virgins of Great-Britain are very much obliged to you for putting them upon such tedious drudgeries in needle-work as were fit for the Hilpa's and the Nilpa's that lived before the flood. Here is a stir indeed with your histories in embroidery! I would have you know, that I hope to kill a hundred lovers before the best house-wife in England can stitch out a battle, and do not fear but to provide boys and girls much faster than your disciples can embroider them." A love of true, unsophisticated nature was proclaimed, concluding: *"Without minding your musty lessons, I am this minute going to Paul's church-yard to bespeak a skreen and a set of hangings; and am resolved to encourage the manufacture of my country."*

The original letter is entirely likely to have been a spoof, giving an excuse for the Spectator to pontificate and provoke with the lofty prejudices of silly men. No doubt the editor had his tongue in cheek, hoping for a response. But when it came, the indignation had all the passion lacking in the earlier passages, and spoke, however edited, in the tones that the Spectator would have heard in homes of domestic bliss and of emancipated fury. A newspaper article does not have to be totally candid to catch a genuine spirit of the times

Patty Polk, a ten year old from Maryland, left us no such doubts in her sampler of 1800. "*Patty Polk did this and she hated every stitch she did in it. She loves to read much more.*" Yet she kept it! Who has not met someone who claims to have hated some lesson in youth, and yet is proud of the learning? Some girls did not enjoy making samplers.

> *"I cannot perceive this business design'd*
> *For anything more than to please a raw mind."*
> Rebecca Nicholson' sampler 1801.

Among families rich enough to afford it, wider economic reasons led to a decline in embroidery, and therefore in samplers. In medieval England, embroidery had been such a mark of heraldry and state, it was forbidden by law to the common people. The law was largely ignored, and there was a deal of embroidery about. Chaucer writes of a young squire whose dress was "*embroidered... as it was a mead, ful of fresshe flowers whyte and reede.*" This embroidery was usually made by the women of the house.

Though Tudor Queens and Duchesses had furnishings made by professionals, the embroidery that adorned their own stomachers, or the vests and gloves of their men-folk, was proudly done by their own royal fingers. Plain cloth cried out for embroidery on bed-curtains, and the hangings that divided great, draughty homes.

By 1800 all had changed. New materials, prints, furnishings, and tapestries were made in factories. Much of the decoration was made by machine. Gowns and dresses shone with silken lustre, bright colours and printed decoration. Ribbons, flounces, cut and fashion, made for elegance that had no need for hand embroidery. Indeed machine embroidery had come by 1851.

White work continued with the needle, so that handkerchiefs, and the saucy glimpses men caught by contrived accident, meant some linen and lace were hand-made and stitched for generations to come. But for the well-to-do, embroidery was no longer a family occupation and their girls began to tire of the sampler.

At private schools, needlework was a gentle accomplishment, like French, dancing, painting or playing the piano. In the adult needlework of rich families, stump-work narrative pictures of the 17th century were replaced by silk paintings filled out with applique and mohair landscapes. Some of these were made by young girls; and when finished with name, age and date, they seem to be a sort of sampler. They were for show, on a wall or a fire-screen; they were demonstrations of skill; they were acceptable family gifts; and they celebrated a coming of age with a name the girl expected soon to change.

In the 1830's, German Merino wool and printed patterns brought Berlin Wool-work to fashionable families. By 1857 aniline dyes had made the fashion brighter. Daughters sewed tent and cross-stitch pictures to give new dimensions to their samplers. The change is obviously mirrored in the samplers of gentle homes for another generation. Beadwork then became fashionable, and appears on samplers, though mainly from France.

The Samplers of girls began with a direct connection to the embroideries of women, yet the two were emotionally different.

Adult embroidery was to be worn out in use; hung in a frame only if it were a fire-screen or a pious admonition; "GOD IS LOVE" or "FLEE THE WRATH TO COME". To add a date and signature would have seemed a childish conceit.

In medieval times devout and noble women were taught to be imaginative and artistic in a life-long enthusiasm. Mary Queen of Scots and her cousin Elizabeth enjoyed embroidery; gave their work as valued gifts; and were proud and patient with the skill.

The Needle and the Pen

Nothing except mathematics is true about everything. "Woman and Girl" does not have the resonance of "Man and Boy". There is such a thing as *masculine*, and in more than grammar. It is different from *feminine*.

Unreasonable prejudice, until quite recently, limited the opportunities of women; yet it was poverty, more often than prejudice, which forbade so many from learning to write. Women who failed to sign their marriage registers do not prove their inability to write. Victorian brides, signing with a "mark", may only show they feared to handle pen and ink. Reading, and writing with pen and ink, was separated in some Schools by extra payment.

Ink was expensive, messy and corrosive. Quills needed constant expert attention to keep the nib trimmed. Pens were kicking, spluttering things. Girls who had not been taught to master these materials, often said they could not "Write". They would not spoil a great occasion by failing to write cursive letters or by blotting a holy document. Industrial production of steel pen-nibs in the 1830's eased some of these fears.

Nineteenth century women of fashion wrote their own particular script, The Ladies' Angular Hand, mentioned before, was taught to gentle girls in school but never to boys. It was cursed hard for men to read, so wives and daughters scrawled it at right-angles over father's letters. This cross-writing communicated to the women of the other household, saved money and preserved secret feminine chat. In their own letters, women deliberately used the scratchy hand to declare themselves aloof from the Copperplate Hand of *Tradespeople!* or the scrawl of gentlemen and scholars. It confirmed a prejudice that Men had made, and made Ladies unfit for employment in any occupation that required writing - which was the point they wanted to make.

This affected handwriting was a hurdle women had to overcome, and very largely they did, with the help of the typewriter.

Men might merit a job that depended on good handwriting, but until the advent of the penny post, few poor women had clear need of the skill outside school.

Yet many poor women *could* write, print letters learned on the slate; enough to chalk a message on a barn door explaining a missed appointment, or to scribble with a bit of lead on a piece of paper. Print-writing was well enough known for them to burn words with a hot bodkin on the bone of lace bobbins. Their mis-spelt messages, "Edawrd" "Love me truley" or "Marrey me quick", show they were literate; only not with pen and ink.

In 1769 Frances Webber's sampler made when 9 years of age, shows the needle was understood as a substitute for the pen:

"An epistle from a young lady to her beloved friend."

"Were paper wanting, or pen to send
My best and kindest wishes to my friend;
Should ever chance all usual means deny

My needle thus should that loss supply.
For sure, Lucinda, they have little art
That want the means to dictate from the heart."

Laura Ashton's book on samplers quotes a letter sewn on cloth in 1693 from a Quaker girl separated from her mother and father.

Dear Mother, my duty I remember unto the and my dear love unto my sister. When I saw my father last his love was unto the but I thought it long before I saw the, but I did my indeavour to rite unto the in more. By they dutyfull daghter, S.F. from Wanstead, the 25 of the 5 month.

S.F was, for those times, fully literate, but she wrote with her needle.

Another such letter was seen years ago among samplers in an antique shop. Its moving and lovely message had been framed and kept. It was sewn early in the nineteenth century, by a woman who had been servant to the wife of her local minister. She wished to write to her mistress who had gone with her husband as missionary to the Windward Islands. She took a piece of fine linen called lawn (because it came from Laon in France) and she sewed a letter on it, well spelt, gossiping and grammatical.

She wrote imagining her mistress among palms and warm seas. She told of her hopes that her friend was well and happy, and how she was still missed and loved back in her old village. The needle was her proper instrument; and thread was the only adequate material for her to write respectfully.

Witney Antiques had a similar letter, sewn in the capitals girls learned in the needlework of poor schools. It was sent, "AS I CANNOT WRITE TO YOU", by Betsy Cort from "Demerary" on the 16th May 1818 to Mrs Wilson.

Mrs. Wilson had returned to England with her husband, having been, perhaps, a missionary in Demerara. It has all the love and sadness of friendship torn apart by unbridgeable distances.

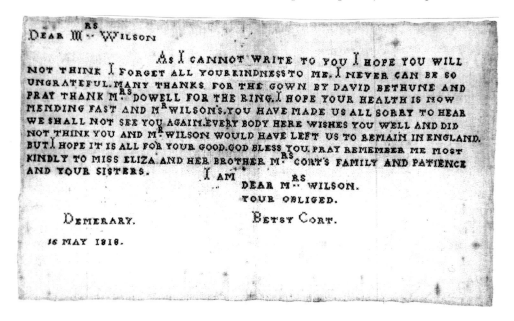

A letter written with needle and thread.
From their catalogue, "When This You See, Remember Me." Courtesy of Witney Antiques.

Forty years on, a woman incarcerated in a mental institution had a mind teeming with paranoid convictions that demanded communication. On pen and paper, her torments would have spilled out almost as fast as thought. But in the capital letters she had learned on her Poor School Alphabet Sampler, Ellen Hey painstakingly sewed her mind onto canvas. Confined and compacted by the slowness of her task, her sentences speak out her turmoil.

Needle and thread for her were not to fashion beauty, nor for conventional and modest show in a sampler. She wrote with them, telling the agony of being poor, misunderstood, persecuted and proud - part Jane Eyre, part Mr Rochester's other wife.

THERE IS SUCH A THING AS A SECOND BIRTH. FOR I HAVE HAD A SECOND BIRTH. I CAN HEAR PERSONS. TALKING THAT I CANNOT SEE AT ALL. THEY CALL THEMSELVES. SECOND PERSONS. THEY TELL ME THAT THEY HAVE. LIVED. DIED. AND THEIR SHELLS. (BODIES) HAVE BEEN. BURIED. ON THIS. HEMI-SPHERE. AND THEY TELL ME THEY WILL. REAPPEAR. ON THIS. HEMI-SPHERE. IN THEIR SECOND PERSONS. AGAIN. AND THEY TELL ME AS WHENEVER. THEY DO COME THEIR PRESENCE. WILL. CHANGE. THE ATMOSPHERE. AND THE ATMOSPHERE. WILL CONSUME. ALL HUMANITY. AND THE HEAT. WILL. LEVEL. THE HEMI-SPHERE. (EARTH) AND THEY TELL ME THEIR SECOND PERSONS. ARE OF THE SAME FIERY NATURE. AS THE 'SUN' THEY INHABIT THE 'SUN' AND THEY TELL ME THERE IS NO SPIRITS. THEY ALL HAVE HAD. BODIES. ON THIS HEMI-SPHERE. THEY TELL ME THEY HAVE. A SECOND PERSON. A THIRD PERSON. A FOURTH PERSON. AND THEY ARE ALL IN THE ATMOSPHERE WAITING. TO CATCH. UP THEIR FIRST PERSON. FROM OFF THE HEMI-SPHERE. THEN ALL HUMANITY HAS FOUR PERSONS IN ONE PERSON ALL ARE EQUAL. ONLY ELLEN HEY HAS SIX UNSEEN PERSONS. IN ONE PERSON. AS SHE IS THE FORE-RUNNER. OF THE MILLENNIUM. CHRIST THE FATHER. TALKS TO US. I CAN HEAR MY OWN. UNSEEN PERSONS. SPEAK. ITS WHAT I WERE SENT HERE FOR. BUT THEY DID. NOT. KNOW. WHO. THEY WERE SENDING HERE. AT SAME TIME. CHRIST THE FATHER. SAYS HE. WILL. RECKON. WITH ANYONE. THAT AS DONE ELLEN HEY. HARM IN HER. LIFE TIMES. THE END. OF TIMES. NEAR. FOR ALL HUMANITY

Ellen Hey's screaming needle.
If asked, she would say she could not write.

Men and women who signed with a mark might be unfamiliar with cursive script and fearful of pen and ink. The typewriting machine was a more effective leveller than education. From offices, women soon sprang into the professions.

Society has restricted the dignity of women, by its customs, its laws, and by assumptions too widely held to defy. History throws up clear evidence that we have not progressed in a direct line from wrong to right. The position of women has fluctuated within social groups as well as in time.

Tudor princesses were taught modern and classical literature, and disputed it with an understanding and respect that would have seemed remarkably queer to the Hanoverians. There were women medical practitioners in Stuart England; women learned in Physick and Chyrurgery and teaching their arts. Women have defended their homes from skirmishers of armies against whom their husbands went out to battle. Books and businesses blossomed from 17th Century women whose activities would be frowned on at the beginning of the next, and approved in the following. In all times women have been the driving force of enterprises whose titular head was a malleable man.

Loss of confidence is as astonishing as the hard graft it is to redeem lost ground.

Chapter 9.

TINKER, TAILOR, SOLDIER, SAILOR

On the Needlework of Boys and Men

In all the long years of domestic embroidery, boys did not make samplers. Some claims to the contrary arise from early samplers where the names of father and mother are prominent because the work was dedicated to them. In some cases the girl herself only signed the sampler with her initials. It is easy to mistake a gift and a dedication for a signature. (see Marcus Huish, p. 85. Cristen Henderson's sampler attributed to her dead father)

Exceptional samplers by boys would be very rare. Patricia Ryan and Allen Bragdon have unearthed two for their American book, "Historic Samplers". Both works are simple Alphabet samplers. George Eisenbrey sewed his in 1826 at about nine years of age. He is thought to have done it as a punishment for impatient behaviour. Julian Chamberlain did his about 1823 aged nine, and was probably incapacitated by illness. Both are obedient, joyless, and undistinguished. Rochester (N.Y.) Museum has one sewn by John Scantlebury, aged 9 in 1923: a fine and completely traditional needlework sampler.

Being a boy is a strong obligation and a great game. Men are able to do very badly the things they wish to get out of doing, and most boys would undertake enormous chores and risk their lives before they would sew a sampler.

A diligent search through thousands of English samplers has discovered four certainly made by boys. Of these, three are exactly as one would expect; reluctant alphabet samplers with rare hints of personal initiative that girls often gave when restricted to the same pattern. Isaac Fitton in 1818 throws in a couple of hearts but finishes when only a third of his canvas had been used. Arthur Webb aged eleven at Nazing School sewed the strawberry border, two capital and one cursive alphabets, before ending, "*Thy will be done*". Perhaps he worked it in the school infirmary. The date, 1873, seems to have been added later. The omission of j in two alphabets suggests he was copying an older sampler.

Robert Nimmo's in 1848 was a task of no more than a week or two, as unlovely as any, and less poignant than the pitiful samplers of poor girls. What circumstance drove him to it?

In a comfortable home full of girls, some dull winter with nothing on earth to do; no companion and all toys used or broken; bored yet unwilling to read the improving book mamma had bought him; half envying the chat of his sisters busy with their samplers; perhaps he slighted their simple work. Challenged that he was only jealous because of his inability, he would be sure to boast he could do it as well as they if only he cared to. And his sisters would scorn him unless he proved his boast.

What other constraints would make a boy attempt such a "girly" thing?

Illness perhaps? A long weakness that forbade running, jumping, kicking a ball about or climbing trees?

A father so angry at his lazy disobedience that he forced the humiliation on his son?

Did he do it, knowing that it was the only way back to a world where it would not be expected ever again? Whatever the cause, he made it; one of three swallows that never made a summer.

That leaves one boy's sampler that stands out against these assumptions. James Wilson sewed his sampler aged 12 in 1838. It can be found in Haslemere Museum along with Isaac Fitton's.

James' work has all the meticulous care and traditional patterns expected from an affluent and dedicated girl. The verse is a version of seventeenth century samplers and one rarely used during the intervening hundred years.

James Wilson is my name and with my needle I mark the same.
And by my work you may see what Pains my Parents took with me.

There are no alphabets and the enthusiastic motifs speak of past times. Perhaps it was sewn copying earlier samplers in the family. The birds and insects have an antique feel; the squirrels and the bird under a weeping willow recall memories of Ackworth.

A Boy's Sampler, Robert Nimmo, 1848.

James Wilson's sampler.
Courtesy of Haslemere Museum.

Of course, many men used the needle, but adult needlework is entirely another matter. Women's domestic embroidery was traditional, and girlish samplers grew from a natural record of work into rituals for a particular period in life. Boys would be apprenticed to the needle as a trade; it was never part of their home life or their schooling.

Men embroidered, skilfully, not for love of it but for money. Successive court embroiderers were male, and so were many workers in the early Broderers' Guilds.

In the seventeenth century, chapmen went around the country selling slips of embroidered emblems, so that women could cut them out and sew them into their domestic embroideries. Repetitive stags, butterflies, snails, monarchs sitting under trees, hunting hounds with bells on their collars, and couched and grinning lions, were spaced about the canvas and filled in with flowers and personal stitching to make stump-work pictures for workboxes. Perhaps the slips were made by men - certainly they were industrialised needle-works, not domestic.

Perhaps as a consequence, that kind of embroidery was the first to be mechanised. In the middle of the 19th century silk pictures, portraits and advertisements began to be produced in factories. Sentimental poems were machine-stitched for greetings; silk flags, regimental badges, and posies of flowers were included in cigarette packets to encourage commercial loyalty. During the First World War British soldiers sent home patriotic silken postcards, machine-made in France and finished by French girls with sentiments of longing and love.

Long after the fashion of childhood samplers had ended, slips like 17th century haberdasheries were produced for blazer badges, for the pips on a Lieutenant's shoulders, and the albatross wings on a pilot's breast.

And of course, tailors were men. We learned in the nursery that they sat cross-legged for their work; not like seamstresses, milliners or embroiderers on a stool or chair. They made the jackets, breaches, suits, coats, and cloaks of their day; coarser cloth than a woman's dress, with stiffening through which the needle had to be forced. Upholstery also was often a man's work. Whitework, dresses, and all domestic sewing was largely the province of women, but Shakespeare's father made gloves. Many were later, no doubt, embroidered by the women who bought and gave them as presents to their men.

Leather work of all sorts was sewn by men, with awls and heavy waxed thread.

Cordwainers made boots and shoes; saddlers fitted the harness tackle for carts and horses. Bodkins and needles were tools for women and men. The dividing line seems to be the toughness of the material, and the power needed to force the point.

Otherwise men took up the needle, perforce, in the armed services, because they had no women to do it for them. In two Great Wars they were issued with a "hussif", the only housewife they had, to cobble holes in their socks, or to sew on buttons. Where the needle was not unknown, male embroideries were made, in unusual circumstances:

Soldier service had its long hours away from the comforts of home or anything sensible to do. Soldiers on the India stations made tapestries of their regimental badges. Others made patchwork quilts. Soldiers, convalescent from wounds or illness, overcame the tedium of it with a sedentary and time-consuming activity.

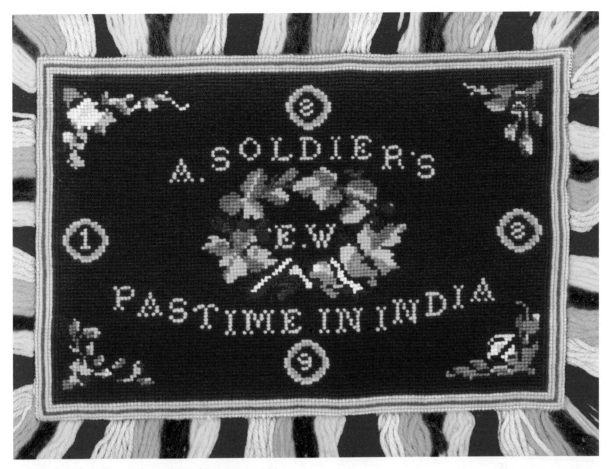

A soldier's woolwork from the India station. 1889

A similar kind of embroidery erupted suddenly in the British navies of the nineteenth century. It became a strong tradition among sailors, and disappeared after the Great War. For a time these "Long-wool" works, dusty, neglected and cheap, appeared among embroidery and textile sales of women's work. They are now valued, rare and interesting.

During great sea voyages, sailors spent long, tedious hours with nothing seamanlike to do. They scratched scrimshaw pictures on walrus ivory and the teeth of sperm and killer whales. They did it on conch shells too, working through the outer shell to expose the mother-of-pearl inside. These mementoes would be carved by sailors whose trade made them familiar with sharp tools.

One sailor pared a foot long lath of whale-bone to serve as the busk of his sweetheart's corset. Very elegantly at either end he outlined himself as a jaunty sailor and his pretty love, demure and curled in her best dress. Between, sailed his tall three-masted ship, attendant boats and a tall-funnelled early paddle boat tug.

It was a token of saucy affection that would hug his sweetheart as intimately as he would like to do; a present and a token of love.

Ships' carpenters had to shift wooden partitions before an engagement, and plug shot holes, and mend spars and masts afterward. At quieter times, the more ingenious ones would make small toys and models. The tiny square-riggers that sailed mysteriously inside a bottle with a neck too small to accommodate their tall masts must have originated in Victorian times, when the shape and transparency of bottles allowed it. It was a time when steam was replacing sail, and iron replacing timber. A carpenter would have less call for his trade, and more time to fill.

A sail-maker was in the same boat, as they say, and he was skilled with the needle. His strong stitches held the sails together. His great curved needles bound the ropes and mended the sails when they were worn or torn by foul weather. He sewed clothing, awnings, covers; whatever prevented canvas too thinned for sails from going to waste. He sewed up his shipmates, wrapped in sailcloth with a cannon ball at their feet, when the time came to bury them at sea.

When released from these sterner duties, some took up a smaller needle and, on spare bits of sail canvas, made woollen tapestries of seas and ships and foreign shores. The impetus for this embroidery came with the transformation of ships to steam power and the change in construction from oak to iron.

By 1864, the Red White and Blue squadrons were ended, and the White and Red ensigns began to distinguish the Royal from the Merchant Navies. The Blue remained for private yachts. Sailors' Long-wool work continued in all the navies. In earlier examples the chequered lines of gun ports may have been sewn on a ship showing the red ensign, but merchant ships of the day also carried cannon.

Sailor's Long-Wool Work. A two gun-deck warship. C.1850

The reverse of the previous work.

Sailor's Long-Wool work. A merchantman schooner, c.1860.

Nostalgia for the glory days of sail tempted sailors to depict the old wooden square-riggers when history could easily see their days were ending. Turner's famous picture, the sad hulk of the "Fighting Temeraire" being towed to the breakers yard by a smoke-stacked tugboat is an epic of the time.

Tea clippers were the sail-makers' last employment on square-rigged vessels. Old salts took berth in private yachts and fishing smacks; and later, in the sail-less and gun-turreted ironclads of the Navy. The old traditions of making Wool-work pictures continued.

The tradition was honoured and strong, though it lasted less than a hundred years.

To make the best use of wool, sailors anchored long stitches at either end. The satin and other embroidery stitches of women repeat the design on the back of the cloth, where the picture is recognisably reversed. Since sailor works were designed to be seen only from the front, like the Bayeux tapestry, what appears on the back is often not even a ghost of the front. Victorian sailors searching for economy had discovered for themselves the Bayeux Stitch that Saxon women had used nine hundred years before.

Sailors used cotton thread to show rigging and other familiar details. At least one wool-work of an iron-clad troopship, c 1870, was sewn by a soldier from the Essex Regiment. The needs of the British Empire put red-coats on our warships and marine soldiers to fight naval engagements as they had done long before Sir Francis Drake.

Sailor pictures were seldom dated or signed, but loyalty to ship and country is often clear. The tradition of making them is peculiar to the British navies, and the earliest dated example was sewn in 1851. Sentiment distorted the images sufficiently to make dating difficult. If a garland of national flags surrounds the ship, the Union Jack with France, Turkey and Sardinia-Piedmont spells "Crimean War". If France, Portugal, Serbia, Montenegro, Belgium, Italy and the U.S.A. fly alongside, the occasion is the First World War. The ship by then would be unmistakeably an iron-clad.

Coloured illustrations
A long-wool work commemorating the Crimean War.

From the top the left hand flags are; Union flag, Turkish Flag, Kingdom of Sardinia and Piedmont: from the right; Union flag, French flag, Dutch? flag. The great allied fleet of warships, troopships and supplies that bottled the Russian fleet in Sebastopol was the last such congress of tall square-rigged sailing ships. Some had the funnels of auxiliary steam power that would shortly overtake sail.

Ships of other nations than those committed to the war would be among them. Every commercial nation was interested in the outcome; for the weakness of Turkey and the humiliation of Russia assured that the Black Sea and the Danube would henceforth be open to the commerce of the world.

Though Holland did not declare war, her ships were no doubt gathered among the fleet. When the Dutch were reclaiming land from the sea, the inhabitants of Gramsbergen were disturbed by the rowdy violence of the labourers, and called the village they were building De Krim because it was so like a battlefield.

A unique collection of sailor wool-work can be seen at the Maritime Museum, Sparrow's Nest Park, Lowestoft. Like a reversal of butterfly to chrysalis, it demonstrates the metamorphosis of tall oaken sailing ships to iron and steam; from naval cutters of sail and oars to smoke-funnelled tugboats and trawlers.

Lowestoft fishing smack, with distant sailing warship and yacht.
From Lowestoft Maritime Museum collection, with their kind permission.

H. M. S. Hercules, a transition from sail to steam and iron. C. 1870
From Lowestoft Maritime Museum, with their kind permission.

A Lowestoft Drifter.
By Captain Tom Cook, R.N. one of four embroideries of his peacetime ships, made during his years as prisoner of war, 1914 - 18. From Lowestoft Maritime Museum, with their kind permission.

G. A Henty's Yacht, of Southhampton Squadron. (Half page)
Now in possession of The Henty Society. Made by one of the crew c.1900. The author lived and dictated many of his popular boys' stories aboard.

At the close of Victoria's reign, the British Navy was steam driven, iron-clad and huge. It had fought no major conflicts for many years, and its ranks were full. When the Boer War called for a sudden expansion in the army, sailors were seconded from the navy to serve. Their familiarity with big guns made them particularly useful in the artillery. It is from this circumstance that Field-gun Competitions became a popular part of Military Tattoos for the next hundred years.

The winning participants take a field-gun apart, carry its parts aerially across an obstacle, re-assemble it and fire the first shot. The transfer of men and cargo by lines run from ship to ship was an ageless discipline of sailors. In military tattoos, the "soldiers" are invariably dressed in naval uniform because the tradition began with sailors seconded to the field gun corps. The long-wool work of sailors began to appear with details of the battle-field. The army's formal wool embroideries suddenly took on the picture qualities of a sailor's traditions. Examples are as rare as they are striking.

In 1915, during the First World War, mechanized tanks made their appearance and men were needed to fire big guns from armoured turrets. Sailors already trained for the turrets of ships were again recruited to mount the tanks, and because they brought the traditions of sea service, one of them made a long-wool picture; not of ships, but of an army tank under shell-fire riding over wire and the shell-whipped waves of Flanders' mud.

Boer War. Long-wool work of a field-gun near a kopje.
Most likely made by a sailor seconded to the artillery. Cotton threads meticulously emphasise details of gun, carriage, uniforms, lanyard, bucket of water to swab out the barrel.

The Great War: Long-wool work of a soldier/sailor. c.1917.
Most likely made by a sailor seconded from ship-board gun turrets to a tank.

An uncanny connection links the traditions of children's needlework with embroideries made by servicemen in their time-filling hours. Among the few inscriptions found on Sailor Wool-work pictures are "Remember me" and "For a kind Mother". Separation and the imminence of danger brought sailors the same recollection of love, family, the shortness of life and gratitude that little girls had felt as they worked their samplers.

Chapter 10
TO EMBROIDER THE TRUTH

THE POOR BUT HONEST MAN

Stop reader here and deign to look On one without a name,
Ne'er entered in the ample book Of fortune or of fame.
Studious of peace, he hated strife Meek virtue fill'd his breast;
His coat of arms, "A spotless life," An honest heart, his crest.
Quartered there was with innocence, And thus his motto ran,
"A conscience void of all offence Before both God and man."
In the great day of wrath, tho' pride Now scorns his pedigree,
Thousands will wish they had been ally'd To this great family.

The sampler of Ann Ormrod, 1809.

We weave to elude: a yarn is a tale untrue. Political spin, the verbal trick to make awkward facts more palatable, is probably more to do with cricket balls than thread. Nevertheless, needlework is uncomfortably close to metaphors about deception. The verb, 'to embroider', is a metaphor for something discreditable. It is a plain tale with something added to hide a fault; a deception, to embroider the truth.

It was not always so. Back in the antique dawn of civilised life, the white hands of young girls pulled and twisted wool as it came off the distaff. To preserve her soft and nimble fingers, she did no washing of clothes or other rough work. The rough hands of mature women caught the fibres of the wool and ruined the evenness of the thread. So spinning was a valuable task befitting young maids - spinsters as they were called. Lanolin anointing fingers from the running thread, moistened the natural smoothness of young skin. From such old prejudices came the legend of Isolde de Blanche Mains.

Spinning was done standing up. Greek pottery is decorated with pictures of girls, standing, sinuous in doorways; a distaff at the right shoulder and the left hand spinning and throwing the spindle. Young men searching for a wife came to see; and she held her head high, for she knew, as a girl does riding a horse, that the pose set her off most beautifully. Spinning and courtship went together.

Remember the girl whose mother said she could spin so finely she spun straw into gold? Rumplestiltskin rescued her from misery but was thwarted of his payment and she married her prince. The myths go on and on. Remember Sleeping Beauty? Did she eat a poisoned apple or prick her finger on a poisoned needle? She also got her prince. The spindle had a sharp point. Was she spinning or sewing? Either way, the myths made a path to find a husband!

Remember Penelope who kept unwanted suitors at bay by unpicking her embroidery each night? Odysseus came, at last, to the ancestral home with his son, to save her and to slay all his rivals. Embroidery was a royal and a beautiful and a virtuous thing to do.

Philomel had her tongue cut out by the man who raped her. Unable to accuse him, she painfully pictured the whole assault in embroidery, and he was condemned. In reward for her persistence, the gods changed her into the nightingale.

Samplers are as old as embroidery. In 1546 they were valued enough to be given in wills. Margaret Tomson left, "*Alys Pynchebeck, my systers doughter, my sawmpler with seams.*" They are mentioned in English literature by Skelton, Sydney, and Barnabe Riche who described how they were used when deciding what emblems to sew into a new work.

Shakespeare mentions them more than once. He must have seen two girls together, sewing both ends of the same cloth. He knew samplers to be significant of the loss of friendship and innocence during the transition to womanhood.

In A Midsummer Night's Dream, Helena says:

> *"O, is all forgot? All schooldays' friendship, childhood innocence?*
> *We, Hermia, like two artificial gods, have with our needles created both one flower."*
> *Both on one sampler, sitting on one cushion,*
> *Both working of one song, both in one key,*
> *As if our hand, our sides, bodies and minds had been incorporate."*

When used to embroider heraldry, the needle was a political instrument. In the Bayeux Embroidery, Saxon fingers promoted the Norman view of history.

Long before the Reformation, it was a moral instrument. Emblems of saints and the cross, decorated copes that popes accepted as gifts, valued as the special art of the English. The texts that replaced them after the Reformation, seemed then too pious for every taste; and heavily religious texts, today reduce the market value of samplers.

In the "City Match" by Jasper Mayne, 1639, a man complains of his wife's excessive piety and education:

> *"She is a Puritan at her needle too …*
> *She works religious petticoats; for flowers*
> *She'll make church histories. Her needle doth*
> *So sanctify my cushionets; besides,*
> *My smock-sleeves have such holy embroideries*
> *And are so learned, that I fear in time*
> *All my apparel will be quoted by*
> *Some pure instructor."*

In contrast, the commonplace charm of the following verse brings a smile to our faces, and touches our hearts with recognition:

> *"My work's composed of black and white, And various colours, somewhat bright.*
> *It is but small for I am young, Slow moves my needle, fast my tongue.*
> *The days are long, the weather hot, Sometimes I work and sometimes not.*
> *Seven years my age, thoughtless and gay, And often much too fond of play."*
> Sophia Mitchell's sampler, 1807

With affection women are called gossips. Many little girls are called chatter-boxes. Sir Thomas Moore loved his daughters dearly but wrote to them that they were "*prattlers by nature*". If there was ever truth in such observations, they were justified in the sewing circle. These were little republics, where talent not rank ruled, and mutual help, and respect for old arthritic fingers, and encouragement for the young.

While needles were busy, the mind could wander over everything in the world, and tongues would wag happily. Though their samplers are so different, that much was the same for the rich and the poor.

What has been written about the fearsome aspects of God's Justice lost conviction at the end of the eighteenth century. Faith came to rely on repentance, and the mercies of a gentler God who understood childish faults. This change in sampler verse appears as Romanticism replaced Reason in literature.

The desire to erase all terrors resulted in some overly plush verses, smothering reality with cloying sweetness. The attempt would not have prevailed against whispers that gather in the corners of playgrounds; the "truth" that grown-ups do not want us to know. One sampler imagines the baby brother of a twelve-year old had recently died:

Mother what is Death?
"Mother, how still the baby lies! I cannot hear his breath;
I cannot see his laughing eyes - They tell me this is death.
My litle work I thought to bring, And sat down by his bed
And pleasantly I tried to sing - they hushed me - he is dead.
They say that he will rise again, more beautiful than now;
That God will bless him in the skies - O, Mother, tell me how!"
"Daughter, do you remember, dear, the cold, dark thing you brought,
And laid upon the casement here, - A withered worm you thought
I told you that Almighty power could break that wither'd shell,
And show you, in a future hour, something would please you well.
Look at the chrysalis, my love, - And empty shell it lies; -
Now raise your wandering glance above, To where yon insect flies!"
"O, yes, mama: how very gay Its wings of starry gold!
And see, it lightly flies away beyond my gentle hold.
O, mother, now I know full well, if God that worm can change,
And draw it from its broken cell, on golden wings to range. -
How beautiful will brother be, when God shall give him wings,
Above this dying world to flee, And live with heavenly things!"
                Sarah Ann Ley's sampler, 1842

That which is acceptable changes with time. The old ghoulish images endured:
"In the cold Grave this Frame must rest
And worms shall feed in this poor Breast
These Hands shall then be Useless grown
And I alas no more be known
No more these feet shall ever walk
No more this Tongue shall ever talk."
                Ann Thomas' Sampler, 1863, Swansea Valley, West Glamorgan.

Elsewhere the Stoic messages of Writing Masters bred so strong an influence that fathers imposed a Humanist philosophy on their daughters. The consolations of the Church, and the values of polite society are equally rejected by the brave verse Mary Kitchen sewed on her sampler in 1838.

> *"I envy none their pageantry and show; I envy none the gilding of their woe.*
> *Give me, indulgent gods, with mind serene, And guiltless heart, to range the sylvan scene.*
> *No splendid poverty, no smiling care, No well-bred hate or servile grandeur there;*
> *On every thorn delightful wisdom grows; In every rill a sweet instruction flows."*

It is a sentiment older than the Forest of Arden, where the Duke speaks of tongues in trees and sermons in stones. (*"As You Like It"*). Few schools would dare let their girls copy such a verse. It is worth noticing because it is unusual, individual, satirical and bold; dignity devoid of embroidery and short on hope. One hopes that Mary had the character to wear it well. The prejudices that look upon childhood change with time; so do those that look on men and women.

The feminine traditions, assumptions, and sentiments of samplers were set in the eighteenth century within well-to-do families. As the conditions and expectations of poor girls is described, the background of affluent women needs to be understood to appreciate what they sewed and what they wrote in their samplers. That century was more certain than the one before or after, that men were by nature to rule women.

Wealthy women were denied a schooling that matched their intelligence and critical judgement. Greek and Latin were thought as inappropriate as commercial technology or mathematics, so the conversation of learned men was shut from women until Homer was translated. Worse! Polite society believed women to be congenitally frivolous and easily captivated by appearances, with a natural interest span too short to grasp anything of a depth easily fathomed by men. No wonder then, women married to sturdy husbands fell in with the convention that their interest was limited to dress and entertainment, and their reading to scripture or idle romances: if they were refused sympathy, they might get a gown by pandering to the condescending prejudices of men.

The sentiment that motivated most samplers was composed of dedicated faith in one Christian God and to the ordered rules of leisured and genteel society.

By 1863 samplers had started to go quite out of fashion, and beyond the plain-clothes samplers of the Poor School curriculum, families continued them only in the Celtic fringes of Britain. That year, in the Isle of Man, Catherine Crellin sewed a hope of heaven that had sustained nearly every little needle-woman since samplers began.

> *"When I can read my title clear To mansions in the skies,*
> *I'll bid farewell to ev'ry fear And wipe my weeping eyes.*
> *O grant me, Lord, till life is past, At Jesu's feet to abide;*
> *So shall he lift me up at last, And seat me by his side."*

Samplers dominated by the English style were made in the Celtic fringe. The Englishing of Wales and Ireland did not result from a tide of Anglo-Saxons arriving when the Romans left. Military dominance of medieval times; economic richness of agriculture over lands more suitable to cattle or sheep farming; and an "English" seat of government and preferment weakened the grip of ethnic traditions. The linguistic dominance of Poor School English confirmed these influences in the nineteenth century. Most Welsh samplers, if not from in-coming English families, come with styles traditional among the English.

The Map Samplers of Welsh schools now and then sewed only outlines of the principality. Their maps tend to be simpler, and in wool rather than silk. Irish and Scottish schools mostly made maps of their own countries and counties. The United Kingdom had ways and cultures not entirely English.

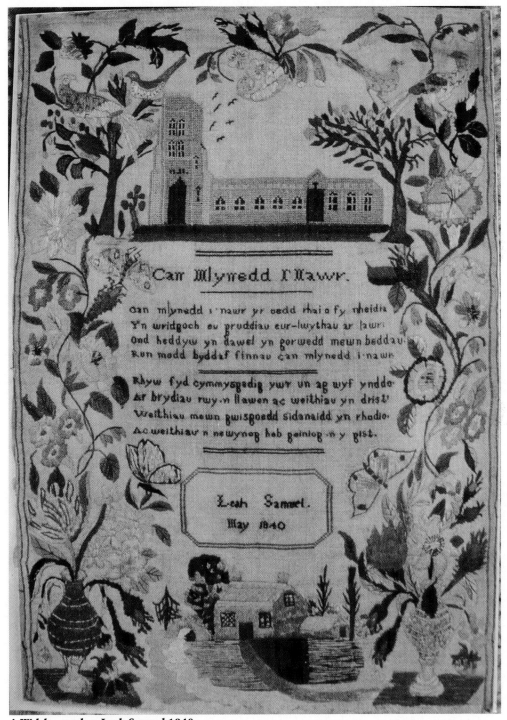

A Welsh sampler. Leah Samuel 1840.
Courtesy of St Fagans National History Museum, Cardiff.

Margaret Crellin, Peel, 1810. A sampler from the Isle of Man.
Courtesy of Manx National Heritage, The Manx Museum, Douglas

Chapter 11
CELTIC AND SCOTTISH SAMPLERS

While thus my fingers on the sampler rove,
The letters form or teach the flower to blow,
O may my soul aspire to worlds above,
And learn betimes eternal things to know.

The sampler of Helen Johnston, Alloa, 1809.

"English" might describe any person who thinks they are; by custom, habitation or birth. It may mean that English is their natural tongue, but the nations that contributed to that tongue are considerably muddled by inter-marriage and political history.

Those the Romans called Britons, Picts, Scots and Hibernians, were Celts who arrived in the ninth century before Christ, and came in greater force with magic iron swords a little later. They overwhelmed the bronze-age people that had lived peaceably in these islands for the previous thousand years. The language of the bronze age has been lost, though their DNA survives, probably from the women folk.

Soon after the Roman Empire fell, the languages of Celts in Ireland, Wales and the Western Isles of Scotland had separated so far apart that missionaries from one to the other peoples needed interpreters. They lived in clans and rarely found kings strong enough to discipline their quarrels or to restrain their habits of raiding each other to take cattle.

Their textile customs were akin though distinct.

They wove heavy tweed and tartan cloth whose design gave it clan identity. This did not invite or need embroidery, for the fashion was largely in the weaving not the decoration.

When the Angles, Saxons and Jutes came and took over, just as the Celts had done before, they ceased to conquer and settle as soon as they reached the end of lowlands that were fertile and easily ploughed. They flowed over the hills, but left the rocks of Cornwall, Wales, the Lake District, the Western Isles and the Highlands to their old inhabitants.

Anglo-Saxons brought languages with a common root. Their languages did not coalesce into a single tongue until they received additions from the Latin of the missionaries, the Norse of the Vikings, and the French of the Normans. The plain cloths of the early English cried out for embroidery as the tartans had never done.

Needlework samplers of the Celtic fringe came to the tradition late and largely by adoption from English migrants.

What these lands did have in common was a life of hardihood, and a kind of poverty that arose from being left only the rocky and isolated parts of the British Isles. It was not the same poverty of spirit that sapped the energies of the poor in English industrial towns, but a proud determination to struggle against the difficulties of finding prosperity by digging in poorer soils.

WELSH SAMPLERS

Before the Reformation, the artistic traditions of Wales and all the Celtic lands were joined with England by the universality of the Catholic Church. Inside the church, embroidery was spoken off with as much pride and understanding as it would have been in England. A poem written in Welsh by Gruffudd ab ieuan ap Llewelyn (c1470 - 1535) expresses this clearly. Its translation is:

"Incomparable art thou in thy land and infallible thy skill, if thou dost weave fine silk just as the nuns do today. Work, O girl, with thy slender white hand at the task of all London's women. Thou art one who would make birds with a needle - Place it on the bench as an instruction to young people. The learning that by God's grace has been bestowed on thee, turn into an education for them."

It speaks of the earlier tradition when the sampler was an exemplar, not the party-piece of young girls in Protestant secular society.

The considerable collection of Welsh Samplers housed at St. Fagan's National History Museum, Cardiff CF5 6XB, shows no white-work samplers except English ones, and no Welsh samplers of the 17th century. There are few from the 18th century and many of the earliest are either English or seem to have been influenced by visitors from England.

This confirms the impression that there was no native tradition of sampler making in Wales. Those from private schools are distinguishable from the English tradition only by specific Welsh emblems. Welsh pride in their nationality was strong enough; but sampler making was not their natural medium for expressing it.

From 1803 is a Map Sampler of Wales. The canvas and wool thread shows the maker not to be rich, yet the design suggests she was not at a Poor School. From 1804, another sampler shows the allegorical figure of "Wales", with a goat, the Prince of Wales' feathers and a leek. In 1808 Jane Morgans from Carnavon described the history of Wales and named her counties in a Text Sampler. She finished: *"The Welch are Honest, Brave, & Hospitable"*.

One sampler shows Welsh dragons, and in 1821 a verse from the Welsh Bible is followed by its English translation. Poor Schools and the state Board Schools taught in English and discouraged the use of Welsh, so the language never appears in their needlework. Homes and private schools were free to support a language that was fast losing economic advantage. A rare instance is the sampler of Leah Samuel, 1840, which pictures a church and a cottage, with this verse:

"Can Mlynedd I Nawr
Can mlynedd I 'nawr yn oedd rhai o fy nheidiau
Yn Wridgoch eu gruddiau eur-lwythau ar lawr
Ond heddiw yn dawel yn gorwedd mewn beddau
Run modd byddaf finnau can mlynedd I 'nawr.

Rhyw fyd cymmysgedig yw'r un ag wyf ynddo
Ar brydiau rwy'n llawen ac weithau yn drist
Weithau mewn gwisgoedd sidanaidd yn rhodio
Ac weithou'n newynog heb gainiog 'n y gist.

A hundred years from now, my sturdy forebears gave
In grief and pain, Life's grim and certain due.
Yet calm forever now they take, within the grave,
Their promised rest, as I shall do a hundred years from now.

Our world's a joy that's woven with distress;
Merry, then sad; rich until suddenly poor;
Striding, bold, in luxuriant silk of success:
Then humbled and cold - with the wolf at the door.

(this unlearned translation is the best I can make.)

Jane Game's Sampler in 1865 shows DIARHEBION (Proverbs)Chapter IV, v. 13 in Welsh, and an anonymous sampler of 1876 gives part of Psalm 130. Otherwise there are no clues, except the address where that is shown, to declare a sampler Welsh.

MANX SAMPLERS

What was written about Wales, generally applies to the Isle of Man. The island had little industry apart from mining, and in order to improve the opportunities of children, Poor Schools discouraged use of the Manx tongue. Their samplers had the Scots habit of using family initials, and some of their peacocks have a Scottish flavour. But generally Manx samplers are much like the English. The country and its schools were dominated by the mainland.

A correct plan of the Isle of Man was sewn on a Map Sampler from Douglas in 1789, but very few Manx samplers survive from before this time. Most Manx Samplers are 19th century and many from the British or National Poor Schools.

The Manx language is seldom used. One sewn by the mother of William Cannel, perhaps about 1880, gives the Lord's Prayer in Manx:

"*Ayr ain t'ayns niau.*
Cashrick d(t)y row dt' Ennym.
Dy jig dty reeraight.
Dt(y) aigny dy row jeant er y thaloo mynte ayns niau.
Cur dooin nyn arran jiu as gagh laa
As leih dooin nyn loghtyn
Myr ta shin leih dauesyn ta jannoo loghtyn nyn oi.
As ny leeid shin ayns miolagh(t).
Agh livrey shin veih olk.
Son lhiats y reeriaght as y
Phooar as y ghloyr son dy bragh as dy bright.
Amen."

Another sewn c. 1895, by Eleanor Quaggin Moore, aged 12, of B'Voddan shows:

"*Ta mee er chooilleeney yn obbr. St. John XVII, 4*"
(I have glorified thee on the earth)
"*Ayns thie my ayrey ta ymmodee ynnydyn-vaghee. St. John XIV,2.*"
(In my Father's house are many mansions)

By then the language had so far died in the country that a fear arose it would disappear without trace. If a sampler were ever found using the language of Cornwall, it would indicate wistfulness rather than vigour.

An anonymous Scots Sampler. Bands and a picture showing a Redcoat killing a Highlander.
The sprouting capitals, crowns, Scots Meander band, and the family initials are traditional: the bird on the left uncomfortably like a raven picking on a burial mound. Adam & Eve and the butterfly? Who can tell a child's mind? 16th April 1746 was the date of Culloden, but the sampler is dated 10th of March in the same year. This is judged to be the date it was begun, so it took many months. Peter Law was probably a relative of the sampler maker. Courtesy of Culloden Battlefield & Visitor Centre, Culloden Moor, Inverness.

A Typical Scots Band Sampler.
Ann Ross, from Braelangwell, 1851.
Spartan-poor but well-educated, Ann
lived a hard life. She died within three
years of finishing her sampler, and is
buried in Croik churchyard.
Courtesy of Juliet Nisbet, Perth.

SCOTTISH SAMPLERS

Scots samplers are neither Celtic nor quite like the English. Samplers in Gaelic must be rare. Most Scotsmen are descended from Anglo-Saxons who took the lowlands to the South of Perth and left the West Coast, the Highlands and Islands to the Celts in the sixth century. They spoke a dialect of English that a thousand years later became the language of Robert Burns.

The Saxon city of Edwinsburgh was retaken by a Scots king who had already gained dominion over the Picts living to his North East. Scots kings soon gave up their Gaelic tongues for the cultural and economic advantages of Lothian English. Later Viking incursions, and Norman earls that were invited in to settle clan quarrels, governed Scotland with their amalgamation of English dialect.

After the king of Scotland, James VI and 1st, became king of England in 1603, the British union left a void, aching to be filled by emblems that defined all the peoples north of the Tweed. It was a black hole that swallowed newcomers in spite of roots in England. After Culloden, the self-conscious adoption of Celtic symbolism gave identity to that land; the clans, the plaids and the kilts. Weaving, not embroidery, was their decoration. The Highlands and Islands where Gaelic was still spoken, never had the traditions that gave a reputation to English needlework.

Near the Sutherland border of Ross-shire in the Scottish Highlands, Ann Ross made her sampler in 1851 at her secondary school in the town of Glenross. Her home was in Braelangwell. Her road to school follows the twists of the burn as it descends the glen. Travelling up it, three miles or so may be passed without sight of any soul or dwelling. The trees thin as the glen rises higher, and suddenly, in a valley almost devoid of trees, surrounded by bare hills, the road ends at the church of Croik. No one lives there; and the tough grass that sprouts between hard rocks, springs from wet gravels not deep soils. The church is preserved as a relic of the clearances, and in the churchyard is Ann Ross's gravestone. She died three years after she had made her sampler.

The clearances were the turning out of crofter families from the highlands and setting the hills down to sheep and to the huntsman.

Annie's brother had emigrated to New Zealand, and prospered sufficiently to erect the stone that commemorates the family he left behind. It mentions his father, William Ross; William's two wives, Eliza who died before he married Margaret; two sons named David because the first died before the second was born; two daughters named Helen, and two more named Charlotte; two grandchildren, and Annie.

How hard life must have been in that wasted glen! How tough the persistent hope for survival, and how tragically short of success! The clearances came when Annie was still at primary school, and William remained because the family were shepherds.

Branching from Braelangwell is another glen, and in 1848 all the inhabitants of it were evicted. Their crofts were burnt, and they, heirs to a Gaelic settlement of many thousand years, were left to make a gypsy shelter among the rocks until an emigrant boat should come to take away the able-bodied.

They gathered briefly, with what few belongings highland families had, in the churchyard of Croik, with the church door locked against them. They did not blame the clan chief who had evicted them, but supposed their own incomprehensible faults.

On the diamond window panes that could be reached from outside, refugees scratched messages of despair with their ring-stones.

> *"Glencalva people was in the churchyard here May 24 1848"*
> *"Glencalva, one of the wicked Generation"*

Perhaps the people of Glencalva, making their way down to the coast with other crofters from Braelangwell, were given ship to Canada or New Zealand. Perhaps they lived a better and a longer life once divorced from the hard rocks of their homes; for it is difficult to see how they could have scratched a decent living in those old places.

Hoping they might have fared better does not take away the pain of eviction: Ann would have lost many friends, and found Braelangwell all the lonelier for their going. Her sampler, simple though it is, tells a painful story of struggling poverty.

An old highland lady, who as a girl had walked miles barefoot to school, was asked why it was that, long after it had ended in England, the making of samplers continued in Scotland. "Well," she said, "There was n'a much else to do."

Whatever the truth of that, and she was smiling when she said it, there must have been other reasons. Most Scots do not live in the Highlands.

The school system was not the same as the English, and, after 1860, the Scottish system of standards to mark progress at school included needlework samplers. Many of the Scots samplers from later Victorian and Edwardian times include the name of the school, and the standard of the class when it was made. "P.S." means Public School, what the English would call "elementary or primary"; "S.S." means Secondary School, to which we had no exact equivalent at that time. Now and again one comes upon samplers made at so-and-so "Female School", possibly an exclusively Scottish term.

Of course samplers were made at home, as well as at school, and in the more prosperous lowlands as well as in the highlands. The general making of samplers in Scotland seems to have ended about 1916, like so many, many things did. But the Scots samplers, anyway, had different traditions, and though there was much transfer of sampler patterns across the border, many can be distinguished from English samplers even if no place is named, or the family name is inconclusive. There are obvious emblems, like the thistle, but a surprising consistency in other traditional elements:

Red, Green and Blue: Scots samplers, especially from poorer homes, often have limited colours and shades. But the balance of colours in richer samplers tends to various shades of red and green. Simple red, green and blue, like so many plaids, say "Scotland" in a sampler. The roofs of sampler buildings are more often coloured blue* in response to the general use of slate rather than tile or thatch.

Scots Peacock: The English sampler-peacock trails his tail, walking sideways: the European peacock looks toward you and displays its tail like a fan; the Scots peacock is seen obliquely, and its tail shows a spread six or seven round-eyed feathers displayed. This peacock is found in samplers of the border counties of England more than in the south, and is a motif whose native home seems to be in the Netherlands.

Band Sampler: The Scots kept to the pattern of the band sampler much more consistently than the English. They preferred purpose to prettiness.

Scots Meander: One of the meandering flower borders that were common in 17th century samplers, persisted, often to the exclusion of all others, in the bands of Scots samplers. Its meanders are squared rather than sinuous, and the flower symbols are large, almost completely filling the squared bays.

Crowns and Hearts: Emblems are sometimes reduced to crowns and hearts. Crowns are not uncommon in English samplers, but hearts are, and both are traditional in Scots samplers. When Robert the Bruce died he ordered that his heart be separated from his corpse and sent on crusade. Did he leave behind a special significance in the emblem? Outside St Giles' cathedral in Edinburgh, the stones have been formed into a great heart. Some spit on it for luck, some do not, and none seem to know quite why.

Sprouting Capitals: The alphabets in the bands often include a decorated capital alphabet in which tendrils sprout riotously from every angle and extremity of the letters. The Dutch have a similar alphabet, not met outside these two countries. When this does not appear, the capital alphabet is bolder and more decorated than in English Samplers.

Family Initials: The space not used for bands, alphabets, or emblems, are crammed with family initials; male and female branches. The early Long Band Samplers of the English had used family initials to fill up lines, but the fashion died. It remained a tradition of Scots Band Samplers of the 18th and 19th centuries when in England the practice was rare. The initials or name of the deceased were often rendered in black thread. Examples occur where both parents' names are given, mother in pale fawn and father in black to show he had already died when the sampler was made.*

Fewer Verses: The Scots used verse but not with the English enthusiasm or freedom. Where they do, it is in English, sometimes of the Robert Burns sort.

Real Buildings: English buildings are often fanciful, but when Scots samplers do make pictures, they are more often portraits of identifiable buildings. The traditions of Congregationalist and Baptist Schools in America were somewhat similar.

The sampler of Mary Cameron, made about 1790, is a picture; and it shows the High Street and Trades Hall of Aberdeen. Otherwise it shows few Scottish clues of typical band samplers except the familiar hearts and family initials. In 1878 Mary Myles of Largo, Fife, sewed her sampler still showing the bands, initials, crowns and heart.

If the sampler traditions of Scotland come from Anglo-Saxon roots, why are there so many elements that enable us to differentiate their samplers from those made in England? It can only be from stubborn traditions surviving the union of the two crowns. That avid needlewoman, Mary Queen of Scots, learned her sewing at the French court; but her stay in Scotland was too brief and unpopular with the Protestants to have materially affected samplers for children. During the wars between England and Scotland the "auld alliance" with France may have brought in some continental fashions. Invention, which is notably lacking in French samplers, is curbed in those from Scotland, the home of an inventive people.

The traditional elements of Scottish samplers are clear enough, but it is not surprising to find some of them sewn as far south as Newcastle. On brief occasions between the Viking invasions and the battle of Culloden, Scots armies controlled the north of England: the present boundary from Carlisle to Berwick was never an ethnic or language border. Economic depression brought Scots families to seek their ambitions south of it.

The Origin of Flemish Elements?

When the traditions of childhood samplers were taking form, a new port on the banks of the Scheldt had direct links to Scotland. The old port at Bruges, a centre for the cloth trade, had silted up and only small vessels could approach. Commerce shifted to quays and warehouses further North where a haphazard collection of buildings eventually formed a conurbation called Antwerp.

Artisans and merchants flooded into a town thriving in the new business of Printing. Foreign families, including religious reformers escaping the persecutions of the Reformation, set up home in a cosmopolitan population. Merchants and printers traded in religious tracts, largely indifferent whether they were Protestant or Catholic. The English Reformation was generally Lutheran: early Scottish reformers came, and returned to Scotland with the tendencies of Calvin and Zwingli that gave the Presbyterian tinge to Edinburgh.

Either as merchants or religious exiles, Scots families were living in Antwerp during the sixteenth century, their children mixing with the families and schools of Flanders. In such intimacy the motifs of childhood samplers might have been transferred. Exactly the same pull of trade and religion brought many Englishmen to Antwerp, William Tyndale among them whose English translation of the Bible was printed there. The Judeth Hayle samplers, mentioned earlier, came from Ipswich, a port busy in the cloth trade and with strong connections to Flanders. Edwina Ehrman pointed to Presbyterianism and a similar European influence in the sampler emblems.

Scotland has fewer picture samplers. Scots samplers have their own charms, pleasing to identify; but a sense of economy make their samplers seem dour. Are the Scots naturally dour, or did an excess of Calvinism, with its despairs and damnations, mute their joy?

*Joy Jarrett, who has known many Scottish samplers, identified these significant details.

Elizabeth Death 1771.
A sampler that has hints of Scotland but is far from certainly Scottish.

Elizabeth Anna Sendall, c 1850. Actual Size
Alphabet samplers made very small, just for the fun of it.
Courtesy of Doreen Wood, Baldock.

Chapter 12
THE BIT THAT DOES NOT SHOW

Teach me to feel another's woe,
To hide the fault I see;
That mercy I to others show,
That mercy show to me.

The sampler of Mary Ann Culyer, 1807. (Alexander Pope's Universal Prayer)

Joiners who sold their work used to say, *"Don't worry about the wood that doesn't show."* But they taught their apprentices to make every joint as if the eye of God could see the front and the back of it.*

To discover the character and the feeling of the finest and the best Sampler making traditions, look on the back!

An embroiderer sewing a bunch of flowers in a vase would need perhaps fifteen different colours. Even for a bunch of yellow roses, she must have five to show the curl of leaf and petal.

Olive green for the stem and front of the leaves.
Apple green for the calyx and the back of the leaves.
Lemon yellow for the inside of the petals.
Orange yellow for the back of the petals.
Brown for the thorns.

If she began with Olive silk, it would leave a tail of an inch or so before she made the first stitch. Finishing the first stem she would trail the thread to a piece of leaf, and satin stitch it in before taking it to an adjoining leaf. Half way through that, the thread might run out leaving another trail hanging from the back. Continuing the same colour she would leave perhaps four more tails and innumerable joining threads before the colour was finished. By the time all five colours had been worked, loose threads would leave the back very different from the front. Fifteen colours would leave a mat of threads on the back from which it would be difficult to read the front designs.

---

*Long ago, George Waters taught Woodwork. He was a fresh-air fanatic and always left one of the windows open. We lined up at the end of each lesson to show the task he had set; two pieces of wood perhaps, joined together with a dovetail or mortise joint. He would hold it and wiggle it, making comments on our accuracy. The examination ended with only two grades; acceptable or not. The acceptable he handed back to us: the unacceptable he hurled through the open window. We had to do the task again.

We waited for him to miss, and anticipated a glorious smash of broken glass if he did. But he didn't.

Somehow, the noble certainty of a world where everything was either right or wrong gave dignity to his teaching and to us. Teachers today are not allowed to be so unreasonable, and some of the colour has gone out of being a schoolboy.

Suppose the embroidery was for a bed-hanging on a four-poster. Such needlework might look exquisite from the front, but present a meaningless mess of colour to the sleeper once the curtain was drawn. Most modern samplers are like that; but since they are framed to be seen from one side only, the fault is invisible.

Medieval needlework and the earliest childhood samplers were sewn to a different discipline. Each island of colour was sewed leaving no tails at the start and finish, and no joining threads crossed from one island to another. Stem stitch and satin stitch are the same front and back, so the bunch of roses would appear identical except for being reversed. Cross-stitch does not naturally leave front and back the same but a meticulous needlewoman can make it do so. It was a time-consuming excellence.

Childhood samplers were apprentice pieces to be handled and examined with care, so those old disciplines were demanded of them. Some regiments go to extravagant lengths to prove their parade-ground discipline superior. Some girls at their samplers did the same. Letters of the alphabet stood in their individual colours as clearly on the back as the front of the sampler, and the fact that they were reversed was not a worry. An occasional sampler will be found where a child copied the dedication, signature and date onto a separate piece of canvas; and sewed that invisibly into the back, so that it, too, reads correctly.

All those meticulous cares became meaningless when samplers were made to be framed rather than to be handled. Most sewn before 1720 would have been apprenticed to the old laborious discipline: most after it to the new. Old standards continued in a few rich households, but they may also be found among the poor.

Look for it among the work done in the best schools, whether they were for the rich or the poor.

The needlework of the Quaker Charity School at Ackworth shows after 1800 the same discipline that might be expected before 1700. They read cleanly front and back.

The back of an Ackworth Alphabet sampler. Emma Topham. Courtesy of Ackworth School Estates.

The back of an early sampler; Hannah and Dorothy Edwards.

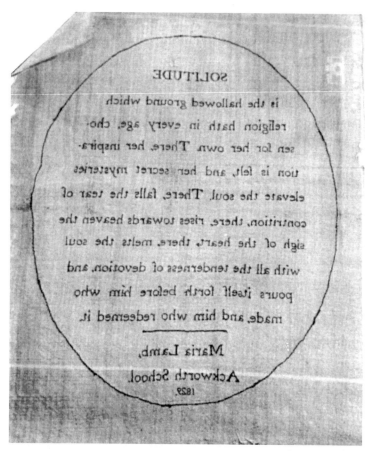

**The back of an Ackworth text Sampler.
Maria Lamb, 1829.**
Courtesy of Ackworth School Estates.

In the middle of Victoria's reign, needlework was a necessity in every home. What was not plain sewing, was learned so that women could make their own dresses. They did it from a rich variety of bright cloths where design and cut and gathers and flounces made each work unique. Embroidery, if it continued, was a very small part of styles that gave personal stamp to women's clothes.

Figurative patterns on cloth came with printed calicos, imported from India toward the end of the eighteenth century. Import was restricted to give advantage to copies from British industry; and furnishing cloths largely superseded embroidery. What remained were needlework pictures, fire-screens, and the mark of personal ownership given by embroidered seats and cushions. It was enough to preserve embroidery as a pleasant accomplishment for young girls. Among men, it found its last flowering in the summer fashions of caps and blazers - manufactured emblems, faintly military in style.

The fashion for embroidered clothes faded, but reappeared on tablecloths, place mats and dressing table sets. It was closer to the sampler border than the emblematic picture at its heart, and seldom included writing. Plain work and Dressmaking dominated school Needlework lessons. And there the subject remained if it was taught at all until about 1960.

The belief then became current that any subject taught at school should be taught to boys and girls equally. Needlework as a school subject died rapidly, and the "Throw-away" society buried it.

Behind these changes was a dramatic transformation of the place of women in society. Before 1950, women clerks and teachers resigned from employment on their wedding. More generally, marriage was for women a full-time occupation, and mainly the wives of the poor worked for wages.

Careers for girls were commonly in unmarried status or interesting interludes between school and marriage. Wives who continued to work mostly gave up their positions to follow their husband's career.

Shopping, washing, ironing, sewing, cleaning and cooking have all been made easier and quicker now. But the advance in women's careers is less to do with time than fundamental changes in society.

Childbirth and cradling infancy are now temporary breaks in the careers of women more often than their end. Within a marriage, both wage earners cannot give priority to the home. Childbirth is avoided more often, and so is marriage itself. Without needlework as a necessary duty, neither men nor women will do it if they can buy themselves out of the need.

Girls are no longer taught sewing at home, nor at school. Manufacture has supplanted the domestic sewing machine. Mending is seldom done. The necessity has passed.

The Art has not.

Many local sewing groups are still busy at the art of needlework for church work where it had been valued more than a thousand years ago. It also lives for love of love, and love of creation. Examples include adult samplers celebrating family feeling, precious memories of home, happy marriage, historic events or the birth of children.

Admiration for antique samplers, decorative tapestry and embroidery contribute to the rebirth of needlework as an art. Notable among these revivals are quilting societies where admiration for North American quilts unites traditional and personal joys.

Those joys are seldom shared in the hobbies of men. Stamp collecting and woodwork are usually solitary occupations. Needlework is a decorative art that is enhanced by working in communal groups. The participants prepare and begin their work at home, and from time to time bring their hopes to a circle of friends. Members of a sewing circle compare notes, chat about their families and neighbours, learn from each other and recognise great talents arising from patient emulation. They revive not only the sewing, but the feel of ancient times.

Their work is painstaking and arduous, but never a chore or an imposition. Competition is seldom acrimonious. Judgement, chance and the inspiration of others are acknowledged. They gather together because they want to. Now and again a man sits in with them. Like girls of long ago with their samplers, they too are making their mark on the canvas of eternity.

BIBLIOGRAPHY

The Manual for Plain Needlework in British Schools, 1839.

Therese de Dillmont, "Encyclopedia of Needlework."

Marcus B. Huish, "Samplers and Tapestry Embroideries" 1900.

Agnes Walker, "Manual of Needlework and Cutting Out", (for use in schools) 1908.

Mrs A. G. I. Christie, "Samplers and Stitches" 1920.

Ethel S. Bolton and Eva J. Coe,   "American Samplers" 1921

Leigh Ashton,   "Samplers" 1926.

A.F.Kendrick, "English Needlework", 1933.

M.Canning Linthicum, "Costume in the Drama of Shakespeare and his Contemporaries", 1936.

F.G.Payne, "Guide to the Collection of Samplers and Embroideries", Cardiff National Museum of Wales, 1939

Mary Eirwen Jones, "British Samplers", 1948.

D. King. Victoria & Albert Museum, Catalogue of Samplers, 1960.

Averil Colby, "Samplers" 1964.

Hugh Wakefield, "The Needle's Excellency - A Travelling Exhibition", 1973.

Albarta Meulenbelt-Niewburg, "Embroidery Motifs from Dutch Samplers", 1974.

P. Clabburn, "Samplers", Shire publications. 1977.

Glee Kruger, "A Gallery of American samplers", 1978.

Naomi E. A. Tarrant, "Edinburgh Royal Scottish Musem Samplers", 1978.

Anne Sebba, "Samplers, Five Centuries of a Gentle Craft" 1979.

Margaret Fawdry and Deborah Brown,   "The Book of Samplers" 1980.

Lanto Singe, "Antique Needlework", 1982.

Karin. M. Walton, "Samplers in the City of Bristol Museum", 1983.

Rozsika Parker, "The Subversive Stitch" 1984.

Carol Humphrey, "English Samplers at the Fitzwilliam Museum", 1984.

G.A.Rettew, W.H.Siener & J.T.Wass, "Behold the Labour of my Tender Age",
                    Rochester, (NY) Museum and Science Center,   1984.

Jutta Lammer, "Making Samplers", New and traditional designs, 1984.

Sarah Don, "Traditional Samplers", 1988.

Muriel Best, "Stumpwork". 1987.

Dr Janet West, (Nautical Woolwork Pictures) Antique Collecting Journal 22/8/88; (Sailor Woolwork Pictures), The Mariner's Mirror 85/1/99.

Xanthe Brooke, "Men, Birds, Beasts & Flowers", 17th C. design sources, Exhibition catalogue.

L.S.Garrad & Y.M.Hayhurst, Samplers in the Collection of the Manx Museum. 1988.

Judith Reiter Weissman & Wendy Lavitt, "Labours of Love", (American) 1988.

Christine Stevens & Mair Ross, "Samplers from the Welsh Folk Museum Collection," 1991.

Rebecca Jarrett Scott, "An A - Z of British 18th and 19th Century Samplers." 1993.
Joy & Stephen Jarrett, Rebecca Scott; Witney Antiques' Catalogues - A School Room Exercise, House & Garden, All Creatures Great and Small, Town & Country, How Fragrant the Rose, Upstairs-Downstairs.   Plain & Fancy, Paradise Revisited, When This You See Remember Me, Diligence, Industry and Virtue; An Exceptional Endeavour.
Dorothy Bromiley Phelan, "The Point of the Needle". A Dorset Exhibition 2001.
Patricia Ryan & Allen Bragdon, "American Historic Samplers" Check title, date etc.

For the Origins of Sampler Texts

Almost anywhere in English Literature, sacred and profane. Particularly:
The Bible, Apocrypha and Prayerbook in English; c. 1530 etc.
Popular childhood books such as Horn books, Battledores, Primers, and "A new Riddle Book for Good Boys and Girls, John the Giant Killer, 1778.
Francis Quarles, "Emblemes", 1635
John Bunyan, A Book for Boys and Girls, or Country Rhimes for Children," 1686.
Isaac Watts, "Divine Songs attempted in Easy Language for the Use of Children", 1720.
John Gay, "Fables", 1736.
Alexander Pope, his works in general; particularly Essay on Man, Moral Essays, Universal Prayer.
Wayland Johnson Chase, "The ARS MINOR of Donatus" 1926, Wisconsin University Studies.
Richard Runciman Terry, "The Scottish Psalter of 1635", 1935.
Harvey Darton, "Children's Books in England", 1932.
Rosemary Freeman, "English Emblem Books", 1948.
Claudia N Thomas, "Alexander Pope and his Eighteenth-Century Woman Readers, 1994.

Where Samplers may be seen

There are specialist Sampler auctions in the great London sales, and they crop up often in most provincial auction sales. It is worth looking for them in Antique Fairs and shops. To be sure of seeing them, it is necessary to go to particular museums and grand houses.

Notable collections and sales in the United Kingdom are listed in:-
Sampler Directory of the UK from The Sampler Guild.
19 York Road, Maidenhead, Berkshire. SLG6 1SQ
www.thesamplerguild.co.uk